PAIN

THE DIVINE MYSTERY

WHY GOD ALLOWS SUFFERING

ELMER L. TOWNS

Pain—The Divine Mystery: Why God Allows Suffering
by Elmer L. Towns
10 digit ISBN: 0-7684-0513-0
13 digit ISBN: 978-0-7684-0513-2
Ebook ISBN: 978-0-7684-0514-9

DEDICATED TO OUTSTANDING

MEDICAL DOCTORS

WHO HELPED ME THROUGH MY

STRUGGLE WITH CANCER:

DR. CHARLES J. CATALANO, MD
Gastroenterology

DR. WILLIAM KITTRELL, JR., MD
General Surgery

DR. JOHN MACNEILL, MD
Oncology

CONTENTS

PREFACE: Enigma: Pain, a Divine Mystery.................................7

INTRODUCTION: Pain I Thought I Couldn't Endure...........13

Section One:

WHEN YOU HURT

1. PURPOSE: The Divine Sculptor Chisels on You

   for a Purpose...21

2. WHY PAIN? All the Wrong Reasons to React to Pain........27

3. WHY NOT PAIN? The Many Results of Pain.....................33

4. COPING: Your Reaction to Pain...................................41

Section Two:

THE WORST THING THAT COULD HAPPEN

5. HELPLESSNESS: A Hospital Makes You Feel

   Absolutely Helpless..53

6. FEAR: Fear Makes Suffering More Painful.......................61

7. CRYING OUT: The Constant Temptation to Give Up.....67

8. BITTERNESS: When Pain Turns You Against
   Everything and Everyone 71

9. ANGUISH: The Agony of Those in the
   Prison of Suffering 79

Section Three:

WHAT GOD CAN DO FOR HEALING

10. PATIENCE: Mental Adjustment to Living with Pain 89

11. PRAYER: God's Prescription for Healing Prayer...............97

12. FAITH: To Move a Mountain of Pain 107

13. PRESENCE: Nothing Helps Hurting Like Talking
    to a Friend... 113

14. WORSHIP: The Positive Diversion of Pain 119

15. TRANSFORMATION: Suffering as a Change Agent 129

Section Four:

TECHNICAL VIEW OF PAIN

16. PATHOLOGY: There Are All Kinds of Pain 137

17. HEALTH: Health Is the Absence of Disease or Pain 149

18. AFTERTHOUGHT: Where Do You Go From Here? 157

Preface

ENIGMA
PAIN, A DIVINE MYSTERY

Criticism may not be agreeable, but it is necessary.
It fulfills the same function as pain in the human body.
It calls attention to an unhealthy state of things.
WINSTON CHURCHILL[1]

Most of us will leave this life with pain. The cancer will hurt so bad that it presses upon our nervous system until we faint from sheer exhaustion. And then the cancer that has eaten away our lively organs takes one last gulp, and we are swallowed up in death. None of us wants to leave this life in pain, but it is inevitable.

Pain is the road to both birth and death. The comparison is mysterious.

Phillip Yancey in his book, *Where Is God When It Hurts?*, pictures a fetus in the womb: "Your world is dark, safe, secure. You are bathed in a warm-cushioned liquid . . . a murmuring heartbeat assures you that someone larger than you is meeting all your needs. Life consists of simple waiting . . . a fine serene existence."[2]

Then Yancey describes the pain of birth:

One day you feel a tug. The walls seem to press in. Those soft padded walls are now pulsating lively, crushing you downward. Your body is bent double, your limbs are wrenched. You're falling upside down. For the first time in your life you feel pain . . . your head is squeezed flat, and you are pushed harder, harder into a dark tunnel.

Oh, the pain . . . you hear groaning and an awful sud-
den fear rushes in on you. It is happening—your world
is collapsing. You fear it is the end. You see a piercing,
blinding light. Cold rough hands grasp you and pull you
from the tunnel and hold you upside down. A painful
slap—wa-a-a-a-h-h-h-h-h![3]

So there you have it: Birth begins in pain and, just as assuredly, death ends in pain. But birth and death are not the climax to
the story; there's more to follow. Because we have been saved by
faith, death is a doorway into eternity with God. There will be no
tears, no death and no pain. Paul describes it this way: "Death is
swallowed up in victory. O Death, where [is] your sting? O Hades,
where [is] your victory?" (1 Cor. 15:54-55).

And even though we know there is life after death, many
Christians can't quite bring themselves to believe in its reality.
Death will come, but they don't know how, where, or what it'll
be like.

People will be similar in heaven to what they were like here
on earth; except they won't have sinful desires, nor will they be
tempted by a sinful environment. Death becomes the climax for
all that you were on earth, and becomes the beginning to all
you're going to become in heaven. Death is a door through which
we must all enter.

Let's change the subject to ask why must we suffer "senior
pains" as we grow older? Are the senior pains we suffer as we come
to the end of life similar to the growing pains we endured while
young? As we get older our bodies decline: our beauty is replaced
by thinning hair, liver spots dot our face and wrinkles make creas-
es in our beautiful skin. Some try to keep youth with a facelift,
others sandpaper their skin to get a new growth, and still others
use heavy pancake makeup to mask the age that is so apparent.

Why is it that with age we get weaker and we can't work as
long as we used to? Why doesn't God allow us to keep our youth
right up until the moment of our death?

The answer may be very simple. If we stayed young and strong,
who would want to go to heaven? If we stayed virile, stunning,

and desirously young, we'd hate death, fight death and never look forward to heaven.

But God has a timetable in which He has given us approximately 70 years. That's enough time for us to settle the most important question in life: "Why am I here?" The answer is very simple: God put you here in this time of trial to see if you would turn to Him and seek His salvation.

These 70 years are simply the point of a pen, compared to eternity. The pain we have during these 70 years is nothing more than the prick of a pin when we think of the unlimited joys of eternity with God.

Would more people get saved if they had longer to live? Probably not. Would most people do more for God if they had longer to live? Probably not.

Life is your proving ground to reveal what you're really like and whether you're ready to live with God for all eternity. So, if you ever begin to complain about not having long enough to live, get the eternal view. This life is short compared to the length of eternity, so you'll find your question is really nothing more than a complaint.

Let's go back to the analogy at the beginning of this chapter. Death, like birth, is the gift of God wrapped in pain. The fetus goes through all the agony of birth; then the baby leaves a dark womb to enter a world of light. In contrast, think of us being sucked by death out of this life through a dark door of death where we can't see the other side. Darkness scares us, so we are frightened to enter a room where we can't see where we're going. We are sucked out of this life in pain . . . darkness . . . and sometimes with scalded faith. Yes, we believe God even when the scalding water of adversity burns fiercely.

Let's carry the analogy a little further. After the trauma of birth, the little child goes to sleep snuggling in his mother's arms. The child is embraced by love, and the memories of pain associated with birth are obliterated from his mind. The same thing with death. We are sucked through the terrifying door of death into the presence of God. There we are safe in His ever-lasting arms. As we look back on our death, we have nothing but a bad memory. But it won't last long, for God "shall wipe away all tears from our eyes, there will be no more death, neither sorrow, nor crying, neither shall there be any more pain; for the former things have passed away" (Rev. 21:4, *ELT*).

Notice what the *Living Bible* says: "What we suffer now is nothing compared to the glory he will give us later" (Rom. 8:18). Then Paul goes on to say:

> For all creation is waiting eagerly for that future day when God will reveal who his children really are. Against its will, everything on earth was subjected to God's curse. All creation anticipates the day when it will join God's children in glorious freedom from death and decay. For we know that all creation has been groaning as in the pains of childbirth right up to the present time. And even we Christians, although we have the Holy Spirit within us as a foretaste of future glory, also groan to be released from pain and suffering. We, too, wait anxiously for that day when God will give us our full rights as his children, including the new bodies he has promised us (Rom. 8:19-23, *NLT*).

What will these bodies be like? They'll be bodies that will never be sick again and will never die. No more pain!

So pain is the eternal enigma, the mystery that we will never understand. There is no alternate solution to pain on this earth. We'll have to wait until we get to heaven to find out why we suffered more than some, and less than others. Then perhaps God will pull back the curtains that hide the riddle of pain.

We'll see there on the table our whole life drawn out in pictures, words and diagrams. Our whole life will include the acts we've done, the attitudes we've acquired, and the thoughts we thought. As we look carefully at our life, we may see a few miracles, and a few times of divine confluence when God took our efforts and bent them to His purposes. But when we look very carefully at our life on the table in front of us, we'll see it was really a jigsaw puzzle.

Our life is a puzzle. So we spend our life putting the pieces together, trying to make sense out of all our options. Then after death, we turn the puzzle over to look at the back. What we thought were many disconnected acts was really a divine pre-determined plan that God had worked for our life. Even though we did everything according to our accountability, we were always responsible for our actions. Pain that was difficult to comprehend, a conundrum of life, becomes understandable. Thus, the enigma unfolds before us. That pain which we once saw darkly through a glass, we will understand in the presence of God.

Notes

1. Winston Churchill, British orator, author, and Prime Minister during World War II, 1874-1965, http://en.thinkexist.com/quotes/winston_churchill/, (accessed March 2006).

2. Phillip Yancey, *Where Is God When It Hurts?* (Grand Rapids, MI: Zondervan, 1997), p. 265.

3. Ibid.

Introduction

PAIN I THOUGHT
I COULDN'T ENDURE

When you get into a tight place and everything goes against you,
until it seems as though you could not hold on a minute longer, never
give up then, for that is just the time and place that the tide will turn.

HARRIET BEECHER STOWE (1811–1896)[1]

I didn't have any pain; it's just that I had lost all my energy. I was taking a nap every afternoon and going to bed before nine each night. Because it was so tiring, I lost my will to play golf and the slightest bit of work in the garden tired me out.

I had lost my appetite and couldn't even force myself to eat a third of a meal. But that didn't concern me because I had fasted on many occasions—40 days once—and I was used to going without food. But I figured my lack of food had something to do with my lack of energy.

"You have an ulcer," my family doctor, Richard Lane, told me and prescribed me Nexium, and some other medication to relieve the heartburn pain and heal the damage. After three weeks I was feeling better, and Dr. Lane sent me to an internist to have an endoscopy to see if I had healed.

"I don't think you have an ulcer," said Dr. Fred Catalano, who had performed five colonoscopies on me. "I think it's something else." But he was quick to add that both an ulcer and "something else" had the same symptoms.

After the colonoscopy, he walked into the room and said, "You have a malignant tumor on your colon," and then he added,

"I am so sorry to have to tell you this." I wasn't concerned; my previous colonoscopies had revealed nodules that he had removed, so I thought a tumor was just a little bigger nodule. The C word never entered my mind.

When he told me he couldn't do the operation, I asked, "If you had to have this operation, what doctor in town would you choose?" I figured one doctor knows another, and I'd get one of the best in town.

"Dr. William Kittrell is considered by many to be one of the best surgeons in Lynchburg."

Dr. Catalano called Dr. Kittrell and said, "When do you have an opening?" Dr. Kittrell couldn't take me for 3 months, so Dr. Catalano asked, "What are you doing Friday afternoon?" I guess doctors know that they have some "stretch" time on Friday afternoons. So the operation was scheduled for Friday afternoon, Labor Day weekend.

Two days later my wife and I had a disagreement; we had talked about my problem but we had not used the C word. Cancer was nowhere in my thinking but Ruth had listened to the doctor more carefully than I. He had said, "You have a malignant tumor," without using the word *cancer*. So, we decided to find out who was right when we went to see Dr. Kittrell.

"Your wife is right," Dr. Kittrell said. "I am sorry to tell you that you have a large cancerous tumor in your upper colon, and I recommend that you have it removed immediately. You have a tumor the size of an egg attached to your upper colon." He described making a small incision and, using a "cup," he would remove the tumor and I would be out of the operating room in one hour and fifteen minutes.

If I had known about the pain that lay ahead, I would have been extremely frightened. But I was wheeled into the operating room thinking that I'd be out in an hour and fifteen minutes. I thought I would miss one weekend of teaching my Sunday school class, but that I would be back on the job Tuesday following Labor Day.

The operation took three and a half hours, and the tumor was not the size of an egg: it was larger than a grapefruit. The tumor was an unusual type that Dr. Kittrell had not seen before; I was fascinated when I saw this huge tumor. Instead of spreading out, this type of tumor focuses all its poison into the center until it explodes in the body. We caught it before it exploded.

The incision was larger than the small cup he described: it was about 15 inches long and I no longer have a bellybutton! Kittrell described me as having a "virgin" torso, which means that because I had never had an operation, I had never experienced any terrible abdominal pain. I had always been the epitome of good health and abundant energy.

I told Ruth to go on home, that I'd be fine. The anesthesia didn't wear off for three or four hours after she was gone. Then my agony set in. That night, I descended into an abyss I had never experienced before; my pain was so intense that I didn't know what to do. I stared at the clock on the wall that read 11:15 PM; then I prayed, "Lord, help me make it until 11:20."

"I can't stand it any longer," I kept saying to myself, and I measured the night in five-minute increments: "Help me make it for just five more minutes." The nurse said, "Press this button for morphine when the pain gets too rough." I struggled with not wanting to become a morphine junkie. So for about an hour, I toughed it out, thinking the pain would go away. It didn't!

Morphine was the highest bottle on what I call the staff of life. Next to the hospital bed was this tall pole that could be pushed around on wheels. So the top bottle on the pole was morphine, the next bottle was the IV, and underneath was a bottle of something I don't remember.

"I won't do it," I kept telling myself. I wouldn't go for the morphine. But I could feel my will caving in. I felt like someone had kicked me several times in the gut.

Finally, I punched it for the morphine; it didn't help. Then I punched it again . . . and again . . . and again.

Have you ever hurt so bad that you can't sleep? I tried to pray, "Our Father, who art in Heaven, hallowed be Your name . . ." I tried to worship God, but I just couldn't do it. Then I'd pray, "Thy kingdom come in my life . . ." and I faced the inevitable question: "Will I die?"

The pain was terrible, but not terrible enough to knock me out—I wish it had. I kept coming back to praying, "Thy will be done . . ."

"Lord, if it is Your will for me to die, I am willing." When you're honestly ready to die, you might be more yielded to God than at any other time in life.

Finally, I told the nurse about my pain and she brought me a needle full of Phenergan. Technically, Phenergan is for nausea; it's not a sleep aid. But I hurt so badly, I told them that I was nauseous and needed Phenergan; that put me to sleep.

Most Baptists don't believe that God speaks through dreams—but I do. I don't mean that God gives revelation, or gives truth we could only know through a dream. Just as God leads us when we are awake, I believe the dream is nothing more than our recessive memory working in our heads. So God speaks to us in our dreams through the things we plan and do.

I dreamed I was standing in a 1,000-seat auditorium at Liberty University®, teaching students a New Testament Survey class. It was a beautiful new room, super high-tech with PowerPoint screens, and every student had a computer at his/her desk. I was teaching, referring to maps, using outlines as well as pictures, and chronological graphs. It was a wonderful class and I was doing a great job. As a matter of fact, it was one of the most delightful teaching experiences I ever had in my life—except, it was just a dream. Before the operation, I had been working hard to raise money for that classroom, so the dream confirmed to me I would get through my pain and teach in that classroom.

Then I heard the Lord say to me, "You're going to finish writing this series of books that you're working on," and that really built my confidence. It wasn't a one-book process; it was a multi-volume project that included 14 books, and God told me I would finish all 14 volumes.

From that moment on, there was purpose in my life—and pain can be endured when you have a purpose to live through it.

This is not a philosophical book to discuss "Why pain?" although there are some suggestions as to why God allows pain in our life. This is not a textbook for pastors, counselors, and medical people to guide them as they deal with hurting people. This is a book to help people deal with their pain and react positively so that they can grow spiritually through their sufferings.

I have included some other incidences in my life when I had to suffer. And I have done so with the intent of helping others get through their pain.

I pray that God would be with you in your pain, as He has been with me in mine. May the "God who comforts others also comfort you . . . so you can comfort others in pain" (2 Cor. 1:3-4, *ELT*).

Written from my home at the foot of the Blue Ridge Mountains,

Elmer L. Towns
Summer 2006

Note

1. Harriet Beecher Stowe. http://www.quotationspage.com/forum/redirect/myquotations.php?sid=72a34685777fc66d0ab4233fe84c86a1 (accessed April 2006).

Section One

WHEN YOU HURT

Pain is not just an ache in your body. Pain is a murderer and a thief. Just when you joyfully go to sleep, an enemy breaks into your house to steal something precious to you. This thief makes off with your strength or your happiness. But this thief called pain does more than steal; he vandalizes your house. He breaks up furniture; he leaves water running that destroys your scrapbook memories; or even worse, he sets fire to all your valuables. Pain destroys your life. Why doesn't he just take your wealth and steal into the night? Because pain is the opposite side of health. Pain hates you.

Chapter 1 describes God as the Divine Sculptor who chisels away the unnecessary things of life to fashion a masterpiece out of you.

Chapter 2 asks the question "Why does a good God allow pain to victimize His children?"

Chapter 3 attempts to answer that question—but be careful in applying what you read in this book to your life. There are many different reasons why God allows pain—like the many prescriptions at the drug store—not all the remedies are for you. Because Christians have many different problems in their life, God allows different pain to deal with our different spiritual infections and sinful diseases.

Chapter 4 describes your reaction to pain—how you react is just as important as the medicine you take or the therapy given to you because when you realize you're moving toward health, you can endure your pain more easily.

I

PURPOSE

THE DIVINE SCULPTOR CHISELS
ON YOU FOR A PURPOSE

God didn't promise days without pain, laughter without sorrow,
sun without rain, but He did promise strength for the day,
comfort for the tears, and light for the way.

ANONYMOUS[1]

Think of the artist who's going to carve a sculpture of a man out of a block of marble. The sculptor will create a statue that resembles what he has in his mind. So what about you? God had something good in His mind when He began sculpting you.

The sculptor begins with his tools: a hammer, a chisel and a file. The sculptor must chip away at unneeded marble, even breaking up a beautiful section of marble so that it falls shattered to the floor. "Why ruin beautiful marble?" the skeptic might ask. The Sculptor's purpose is not to preserve the tangent pieces of marble in our life, even though they may be beautiful in themselves. God's purpose is to sculpt you to become like Jesus Christ.

Every chip of marble that is cut from the statue seems to produce pain. We don't like it when God takes away our sports pleasure . . . or our food pleasure . . . or our entertainment pleasure. But God continues to chip away, making the marble more like the image He has in His mind. And what is that image? He wants us to be like Jesus.

It seems the more the Divine Sculptor chips away at our sinful edges, the more we complain . . . or doubt . . . or question the Sculptor: "Why are You giving me pain?" "Why are You taking away my pleasures?" Does the Divine Sculptor know what He's doing? Doesn't God have an ultimate plan for our life when He allows beautiful pieces of marble to fall to the floor?

Perhaps the greatest sculptor of all times was Michelangelo, and perhaps the greatest sculpture of all times is his *David*, which is located in the museum Galleria dell' Accademia in Florence, Italy. Of course others will think that *Venus de Milo* is the greatest. However, let's not trivialize over who's the greatest, but let's understand that the greatest sculptor will produce the greatest sculpture.

And isn't God the greatest Sculptor of all? And isn't God trying to make us into the greatest life we can be? As He chips away at our externals, it's much easier if we release them willingly. It's when the pain intensifies and we hurt all the more that we fight the Sculptor. We resist what's best for us.

What I'm saying is that goal-directed suffering is much easier to endure than blind suffering or ignorant suffering. Ask any pregnant woman, and you will understand that the sufferings of childbirth are nothing when compared with the joy of holding her baby in her arms.

Isn't hope a wonderful panacea for suffering? And doesn't the Bible teach that "hope does not disappoint" (Rom. 5:5)?

At my deepest suffering in a hospital room after surgery, my pastor, Jerry Falwell, came to visit me. To cheer me up, he talked about the wonderful things we did when we were beginning Liberty University. He talked about our first basketball game with the students, and our first classes. But I wasn't enjoying his pep talk; I hurt deeply. Finally I said, "Jerry . . . I hurt really bad. Why don't you pray and go?" Later Jerry Falwell told the whole church, "That's the first time I've ever been kicked out of a hospital room." Everyone laughed, except those who understood that sometimes you want to suffer alone.

Byproducts of Pain

A friend asked me, "What was God thinking when He created pain?" He thought pain was the worst thing that God gives to us. He asked, "How can a good God make us suffer?" I'm not going to answer the why question here. You will read that in the "Why" chapter. But I will tell you that God has a plan for the pain in your life. And the benefits that God has are more than the average Christian's superficial response to pain.

The good that comes from suffering is not just the byproduct of pain. For example, a wife said, "My family finally realized how important I was to running the home when they had to do it for themselves. My two weeks in the hospital transformed their reaction to what I do for them." Another byproduct of pain was testified by a former bachelor, who said, "If I hadn't gone into the hospital, I wouldn't have met my future wife who was a nurse."

Those responses are just byproducts, not the ultimate plan of God for the sufferer. God does have good things planned for you to take from pain. "And we know that all things [including pain] work together for good to those who love God, to those who are the called according to [His] purpose. For whom He foreknew, He also predestined to be conformed to the image of His son" (Rom. 8:28-29).

Did you get that part about being conformed to the image of Jesus? God did not create you to just be happy or to just be comfortable or to just live an average life. He created you to conform to the image of Jesus Christ.

Does pain work together for our good? Yes! Pain is good when the Divine Sculptor chisels away excess marble to make us like Christ Jesus.

Two Questions

There are two questions for the Christian to ask about his/her pain. First, "Why am I suffering?" This question is about cause; people want to know why they are suffering. This is a question we can't always answer. The second question is about response: "What shall I now do?" This is another way of saying, "How shall I suffer?"

The first question is not a valid one, although in Christianity people have struggled for centuries with the question of why. This was the motivation for C. S. Lewis's great masterpiece, *The Problem of Pain.* This book deals with the theological and philosophical reasons why we have pain. Technically, Lewis came to the conclusion that God allows pain so that He can minister to His child. So there you have an answer! But it is an answer that doesn't help at all when we're hurting. Would it really help you get through your pain if you knew exactly why God permitted your suffering? Probably not.

Yet, constantly Christians cry out to God like Job, "If only God would tell me personally why I am suffering, then it would be a lot easier" (Job 9:28, *ELT*). Or they say, "I know that pain helps me grow stronger, but couldn't I have grown without this pain?" People want answers from God, yet God sometimes sidesteps their question. God is more interested in our response to pain, than our understanding of why pain comes.

It is not God's purpose to reveal the cause of things; it is God's purpose to reveal Himself. God wants you to know Him, to meditate on Him, and to become like Him. So it is not important for everyone who is suffering to understand the cause of his/her pain. Rather, the real question is how we react to our pain.

Paul wrote a stinging letter to the Corinthians, rebuking them for their outward sin and religious hypocrisy. The Corinthians were hurt by the letter. "So Paul wrote a second letter telling them he was not sorry he wrote the first letter, but he was sorry they had pain; however, their hurt was only for a little while. Paul was glad he sent the first letter because their pain drove them to God" (2 Cor. 7:8-9) (*Praying Paul's Letters,* Shippensburg, PA: Destiny Image, 2008.)

Therefore, suffering is valuable when it produces something good in our lives; it is good when it drives us to God.

Paul tells us, "We also rejoice in our suffering" (Rom. 5:3). That sounds rather foolish to "rejoice" when pain from a broken rib shoots down your arm and up to your brain so that you feel like you had too much ice cream and you have a "brain freeze."

Once again Paul says, "We can rejoice, too, when we run into problems and trials, for we know that they are good for us—they help us learn to endure. And endurance develops strength of character in us, and character strengthens our confident expectation of salvation. And this expectation will not disappoint us. For we know how dearly God loves us, because he has given us the Holy Spirit to fill our hearts with his love" (Rom. 5:3-5, *NLT*).

So what does pain do? Paul says that tribulations build up our character. God is just as interested in our outer man as he is in our inner man, even though the inner man controls the outer. So God allows the pain in the outer man to build strength in the inner man.

Basically, character is developed in pressure, so pain makes us better even though it hurts.

When you go to the gym, the trainer will say, "No pain, no gain." And where does the pain come from? You put pressure on your biceps with barbells; you put pressure on your legs with the treadmill; you put pressure on your back muscles with the rowing machine. And just as pressure builds up the outer body, so too the pressure we get from suffering builds up the inner character.

Think about the person who never exercises but who eats what he wants, relaxes when he desires, and never puts himself in a stressful position. Isn't he flabby . . . fat . . . and spoiled? The person who always has it easy has little or no chance to learn character. So what does God do? He allows suffering to pressure us into biblical character, just as an exercise machine pressures us into physical strength.

Look at Paul the man of God. Wouldn't you like to be like him? Look at Paul the prayer intercessor. Wouldn't you like to pray like him? Look at Paul the minister. Wouldn't you like to have spiritual results like him?

To get the results of Paul, you have to grow in Christ as Paul grew in Christ. Didn't he say, "I die daily" (1 Cor. 15:31)? As you read his biography, notice how often he talked about danger . . . persecution . . . famine . . . hardship . . . nakedness . . . beatings . . . and the threat of the sword (see Rom. 8:24). That doesn't sound like the typical Christian's agenda.

WRAP-UP

Philip Yancey wrote a book called *Where Is God When It Hurts?*[2] That's a question almost everyone asks who is suffering pain. The answer is very simple: He is the Sculptor with hammer in hand who is chiseling away our imperfections. He is transforming us into the image of His Son, Jesus Christ.

Notes

1. Anonymous. http://en.thinkexist.com/default.asp?url=http%3A//en.thinkexist.com/quotation/god_didn-t_promise_days_without_pain-laughter/328078.html (accessed March 2006).

2. Philip Yancey, *Where Is God When It Hurts?* (Grand Rapids, MI: Zondervan, 1997).

2

WHY PAIN?

ALL THE WRONG REASONS
TO REACT TO PAIN

"Pain is hard to bear," he cried,
"But with patience, day by day, even this shall pass away."
THEODORE TILTON (1835-1907)[1]

I was soaking in a hot bath in my bathtub when the phone rang. My wife was not home and I could feel the phone was angry because I ignored it. So I quickly stood to get out of the tub and slipped—and all my 200 pounds of dead weight crashed into the edge of the bathtub. Later I found out I had broken three ribs. The pain crushed the breath out of my lungs, and I crumpled to the bathroom floor. A sharp pain pierced my side when I breathed deeply, so I took short pants of breath and crawled into the bedroom to answer the phone. It wasn't an emergency call, just one of my wife's friends who phoned to chat.

At that moment the pain caused me to lose my sanctification and I angrily asked no one in particular, "Why did she have to call now?" And for the next couple of weeks, I blamed my wife's friend for my broken ribs. Isn't that just like a fallen creature to blame someone else for their problems?

The doctor told me that there was nothing they could do for a broken rib but to wrap it tightly in a bandage, and he gave me plenty of Tylenol to block the pain. In essence he said, "Grin and bear it!"

A charismatic friend of mine called to challenge me with the message from one of my books. I had written a book called *Say-It Faith* (Tyndale House, 1983), which said, "If you have great faith that is based on the Word of God, you can say to your mountain [on this occasion, three broken ribs], 'Be thou removed and be healed'" (Mark 11:23, paraphrase)." My friend told me that healing was absolutely necessary to give credibility for my book. He observed, "God never intended you to be sick, nor did He intend you to have pain." At the time, I didn't question his statement but accepted it, and I tried to pray a healing.

My friend reminded me, "If you can build up your faith so that it is strong enough, you can overcome pain." Then he rebuked me, "You can't be healed if you won't believe in healing." He hit me with the words, "Name your healing then claim your healing."

I prayed but the ribs didn't get better. I even fasted for a day, but still the pain was intense. Then I tried to act as though I were healed, so that God could heal me. I tried to walk straight as though the ribs were not broken, but the big steps of my confident stride seemed to push the needle of pain right into my ribs.

When my doctor invited me to play golf with him, I intended to act as though I were not hurt so that my faith could heal my broken ribs. On the first tee I made an "UGLY" swing to protect my ribs, and the ball squirted down the fairway about 150 yards. I was a long way from the green, over 200 yards. I had a 3-wood that could reach the green when I took a full swing. I prayed, "God help me." I took the full swing, only to clutch my side in the follow-through because it felt as though someone hit me in the ribs with a hammer.

I won't do that again, I told myself. On the second hole I practiced my "UGLY" swing and drove the ball down the fairway about 150 yards. It was a par 5—500 yards—so I needed a couple of big swings to reach the green. I thought about what I did on the last hole and tried something different. The only problem is that I tried to modify my arc but I swung just as hard. Again, something hit me in the ribs with a hammer.

I walked over and sat on the ground, leaning up against the tree. That didn't help, so I laid down flat on the ground and took those short pants of breath to relieve my pain. My doctor examined me and determined he couldn't do anything but give me some more Tylenol. A student of mine went back to the clubhouse to get a golf cart to retrieve me from the golf course.

No matter how hard you pretend that your pain is not there, it hurts. I had even thought that if I continued playing golf, I would stretch the muscles around my broken ribs and the pain would go away. I was wrong.

My wife's friend, the one who phoned to chat when I fell, felt guilty about the broken ribs. She came dancing into the house, singing happy Christian choruses to cheer me up. Because she has a bubbly personality, she gushed with enthusiasm, quoted verses, read a poem, and finally led in prayer. I don't specifically remember what she prayed—it's been over 20 years since the accident happened—but I do remember her asking God to give me a cheerful attitude.

I wrote an account of my pain from my bathtub experience and published it in *Charisma*[2] magazine. That's an excellent magazine that supported what I said. However, I got several letters from readers who said something to the effect, "There must be sin in your life that caused you to suffer this pain." Another suggested, "If you were living in the very center of God's will, God would have heard your prayer and healed you." One even went so far as to say, "Because you are a Baptist and not a Pentecostal, you can't pray in the fullness of the Holy Spirit to get healing." As a matter of fact, Steve Strang, the publisher of *Charisma* magazine, told me they got more letters over my article on pain than any other article that year. So "Pain" must have touched a nerve in the readers.

Still there was another reaction. Our church has two pastors who are assigned to visit the sick and organize pastoral care. One of them dropped by to pray with me. He brought a couple of tracts on prayer, and he even brought "Worship Hymns" on a recording for me to play to help me worship.

The visiting pastor said something that perplexed me: "God must love you because He makes you suffer like this." I didn't see anything about the love of God in my accident. I only saw the soap in the tub that caused me to slip and break three ribs. The pastor continued, "You need to worship the Lord and praise Him for allowing you to suffer this accident." For the life of me, I couldn't bring myself to praise God for an accident. I could willingly accept it in the plan of God, but I didn't think God was responsible for breaking three ribs.

Does God torture us and hurt us until we cry out, "I love You"? I don't think so.

I am Dean at the School of Religion at Liberty University and one of my faculty shared with me his insight: "I see this as an attack from the roaring lion—Satan—who is seeking to devour you." The faculty member went on, "This accident is an opportunity to demonstrate God's power to overcome pain. Let's enter into 'spiritual warfare' to keep Satan from attacking you again."

It seemed to me that my fellow professor looked at my accident through the eyes of Satanic persecution. I didn't see it that way at all. To me there are many accidents in life that are not caused by God or Satan. We don't live in a perfect world. We should expect our share of accidents and trouble: "Man is born to trouble, as the sparks fly upward" (Job 5:7). Again Job said, "Man who is born of women, is of few days and full of trouble" (Job 14:1).

So what did I conclude out of all of this? I live in a world where God allows "thorns" to grow that make it difficult to survive. I live in an imperfect world where accidents happen.

Why do people suffer? I think that's a question that we can never answer because we are finite and limited in our understanding. We do not see the entire plan of God, nor do we understand what He is doing in the life of another. As a matter of fact, we can barely understand at times what God is trying to do in our life.

However, those three broken ribs led to an article on pain. I've asked myself the question many times: "Why do I have to hurt?"

I have a few inclinations, but I don't have the final definitive answer. Different people hurt for different reasons, God has a different plan for different people, and God initiates and works out His plan in a different way for all of us. One of my answers is that God allows pain for many different reasons in the lives of His children, as well as in the lives of unsaved people. While God doesn't cause pain, many times He is trying to tell us something through our pain.

While I was a student at Dallas Theological Seminary in the mid '50s, I attended First Baptist Church of Dallas, Texas. Dr. W. A. Criswell was one of the most eloquent preachers of his generation, having built a magnificent church on the powerful preaching of the Word of God.

While in Dallas Dr. Criswell told the story of one of his deacons who was also a medical doctor. The doctor had a son born to him with clubfeet; the feet bent inward so much that the boy would walk on his ankles if there were no correction. Today as I write (2006) there are many wonderful medical cures for clubfeet, and feet can be straightened through an operation. However, 55 years ago medical technology didn't have a lot of answers for clubfeet.

The doctor built a box with screws and pads, and each night he put the boy's feet in the box. Then he would screw in the pads to straighten out the boy's feet. Using X-rays, the doctor performed many small surgeries to clip a ligament or re-attach muscles. Each evening the boy's feet were screwed into the box as he slept. We know that we don't feel pain when we sleep, but what about going to sleep?

Dr. Criswell told that many evenings the boy would cry and plead with his father, "Not tonight, Dad . . . It hurts so bad." The boy would cry . . . beg . . . and even physically fight his father when his feet were being placed into the box. Nevertheless, the doctor persisted in spite of the pain he caused his son.

Dr. Criswell described the doctor's tears because it hurt him so much to cause pain to his son. The doctor said, "On many evenings we both cried ourselves to sleep." Why did the father hurt his son? So that one day the boy could walk straight and with strength, even run and jump.

WRAP-UP

So what can we learn from this story? That sometimes we are like the young boy reacting to pain. We cry . . . plead . . . and even fight the plan of God because it hurts so much. Yet the heavenly Father puts us in His own divine box to cure our deformities so that we may walk straight, with strength, and that we may even run and jump for the glory of God.

Seldom when we're in pain do we thank God for the box He puts us in. No, not at all. It's only after the ordeal is over that we look back and see the guiding hand of God to make us stronger and better.

Notes

1. Theodore Tilton. http://www.bartleby.com/100/581.html (accessed March 2006).

2. Elmer Towns, "Pain: Who Needs It?" *Charisma*, January 1985, p. 46.

3

WHY NOT PAIN?

THE MANY RESULTS OF PAIN

Pain is inevitable; suffering is optional.
ANONYMOUS[1]

Did you know that a small pain in a tiny part of the body can make you feel lousy all over? One little pain can kill any desire to work, go out to eat, or perform your regular routine.

I was playing golf at the Salem, Virginia, Country Club when I hit my drive under an apple tree. I thought, "A nice, crisp, yellow apple would make an ideal mid-round snack." As I got closer to the tree, I was thinking more of that perfect apple than my golf shot.

I had a good lie in the short grass under the tree, and the limbs were about seven feet off the ground. I was thinking, *If I could make a nice flat power swing, I could punch the ball onto the green; however, I have an up-and-down swing where my club would catch a low-hanging limb.*

I forgot to swing flat, and I swung my club up into the branches. When I powered my club for a downward swing, the club caught on a branch and wouldn't release. My arms jerked backward and the third finger on my left hand was hyper-extended. In between the twinkling of an eye and a New York minute, I saw my third finger on my left hand lay back flat against the top of my hand.

"Ohhhh."

Initially, the mental sight of a bent-back finger sent chills through my arms and shoulders and I thought, *That's so ugly, it hurts.*

For about five seconds I thought, *It doesn't hurt.* Then after ten seconds, "Ohhhh . . ."

A piercing pain shot up from my third finger right into my heart and I dropped on the ground holding my finger as if hit by lightning.

I didn't want the men with me to see me cry, but they knew something was wrong because I was rolling on the ground in pain. One wanted to bend the finger back to see if it was broken. I wouldn't let him touch it. Another had an ice chest, and the ice took away a lot of the pain, but not all.

I tried to play one more hole, but I gave up and rode in with the men.

For the next three or four months, that finger was the king of my life, and I was its royal subject. Everything that finger wanted, I obeyed.

In another sense, that third finger was like a jilted lover: it hurt me every way it could. When I tried to go to sleep at night, I hurt all over my body. When I was wide awake, that pain never let me forget it was there. My pain dictated that I protect the third finger. Isn't that what Paul said, "And if one member suffers, all the members suffer with it" (1 Cor. 12:26)?

I did all the things that you would expect to alleviate the pain. I soaked it in a glass of ice water to freeze away the pain. On some evenings I soaked it in warm water to soothe away the pain. I used four or five different cream ointments to take away the pain, and most of them took away some of the pain. But the whole crunch of pain came back in a little while.

As I write this chapter, it's been six years since I hyper-extended the third finger on my left hand (also known by children as "Tall Man"). I finally got it to bend into a fist as tight as a former clench. There's no pain now. As a matter of fact, the intense pain went away in about two months, but a dull pain lasted for about a year.

Now it's healed, and every time I pick up a tool or use my left hand at a job, I thank God that I don't have any more pain. The intensity of that pain made me grateful for fingers that don't hurt now when I use them.

Why Pain?

Obviously when I hurt my finger, I asked my three favorite questions: "Why me? Why this? Why now?" I never figured out why I went through that pain. Sometimes pain teaches us a lesson or we draw closer to God. But this accident stumped me. I came to the conclusion that it was just one of those accidents that happen. However, I was daily grateful it didn't happen to my right hand. I wouldn't have been able to write for an extended time. Maybe gratitude was the biggest lesson I learned from the hyper-extended finger.

We don't always know why pain visits us in unexpected ways, or at unexpected times. Let's look at some of the following reasons why pain visits us in this life.

First, pain protects us from ourselves. Actually, when you bruise a bone, the pain alters your actions so that you don't continue using a broken bone and the injury becomes a fracture or a complete break. Physical pain shouts, "*Stop!*"

Second, pain strengthens our character, even when most of us don't feel we need any lessons. And what is character? It is seeing life through the eyes of a mature outlook, rather than selfishly living in a world that revolves around our desires. Character is understanding that we must live beyond ourselves, and not just satisfy our selfish whims. It's what James said: "Dear brothers, is your life full of difficulties and temptations? Then be happy, for when the way is rough, your patience has a chance to grow. So let it grow, and don't try to squirm out of your problems. For when your patience is finally in full bloom, then you will be ready for anything, strong in *character*, full and complete" (Jas. 1:2-4, *TLB*, emphasis added).

So James tells us that trouble and difficulties make us well rounded in character. To bottom line our discussion: Character is habitually doing the right thing in the right way.

There is a third thing that pain does for us: it strengthens our faith in God. Sometimes God tests our faith—not to make it weaker, but to strengthen our trust in Him. The Underwriters Laboratory doesn't test products just to destroy them or determine what will make them break; rather, the testing determines that which is good and useful. Then the product receives the Underwriters' seal of approval.

Doesn't Peter tell us, "These trials are only to test your faith" (1 Pet. 1:7, *NLT*)? Perhaps God has put you in bed to see if you will trust Him when pain rules your life. While you have strength to walk about and work, you serve God and love Him; you even trust Him for everything. When pain comes, you must trust God in a new experience never before faced. God wants to know if you will trust Him in the valley of trials as much as you trusted Him at a revival meeting at a Christian camp.

In the fourth place, pain prepares us to serve God better. Look at how God prepared Joseph the son of Jacob to be His servant. Joseph had to go through intense mental and physical suffering before he could become the physical savior who fed the Mediterranean world.

Perhaps one of Joseph's problems was pride because he was Pappa's favorite. "Now Jacob loved Joseph more than any of his other children because Joseph had been born to him in his old age. So one day he gave Joseph a special gift—a beautiful robe" (Gen. 37:3, *NLT*). Now giving a son a coat that elevated him above his brothers might not have been a good idea. The brothers hated Joseph and the coat. Later when Joseph "dreamed a dream" (Gen. 37:5), he made the mistake of telling his brothers. And what happened? "They hated him even more" (Gen. 37:5). Young Joseph was not yet qualified to serve God; he had to learn some hard lessons in a difficult way.

When Joseph went to check up on his brothers for his father, the brothers were both jealous and angry: "Then they took him and cast him into a pit" (Gen. 37:24). When some traders came by heading to Egypt, they "sold him to the Ishmaelites for twenty *shekels* of silver. And they took Joseph to Egypt" (Gen.

37:28). Can you imagine the emotional pain of being sold as a slave—by your brothers?

Remember what happened to Joseph in Egypt? As a slave in Potiphar's house, he arose to a place of oversight over all the other slaves. But Potiphar's wife lied about him and accused him of rape. Joseph was thrown in prison.

Again, Joseph rose in leadership like "cream rising to the top." He became the overseer of the prison. Two who served Pharaoh were cast into prison—the butler and the baker. Joseph interpreted their dreams, telling the butler he would be restored to his rightful position, and Joseph predicted that the baker would be punished for his crime of attempted assassination of Pharaoh. Joseph's prediction was correct.

Joseph asked the butler to remember him and try to get him out of prison. But the butler did nothing until Pharaoh had a dream. It was then that the butler remembered that Joseph could interpret dreams.

Why all these difficulties? So that Joseph could be a better servant of God. At the end of his life, he told his brothers, "You meant evil against me; but God meant it for good" (Gen. 50:20).

Perhaps your pain that you call "evil" is really a tool of God to prepare you for a much greater ministry that you could not have had otherwise.

But there is a fifth thing: pain helps us to empathize with Jesus Christ who suffered for us. It was Paul who told us, "That I may know Him and the power of His resurrection, and the fellowship of His sufferings" (Phil. 3:10). We may have to go through pain and suffering to identify with Jesus, who went through pain and suffering for us. Technically we are not suffering for our sins or for the sins of others. Only Jesus suffered for the sins of the world; but we can experience affinity with Him when we go through our pain.

After I had my successful operation to remove cancer, I found many people wanted to tell me about their cancer experience. When that happened, we had a closer oneness because we both went through similar pain.

A sixth thing: pain awakens us to our life purpose. Why did God put you in this world? Some people don't answer that question until they face death in the hospital. When others go through intense pain, they begin to think of dying, or they think about their life purpose. Paul is reassured of his purpose because of his pain: "Therefore I take pleasure in infirmities, in reproaches, in needs, in persecutions, in distresses, for Christ's sake. For when I am weak, then I am strong" (2 Cor. 12:10).

The seventh reason: our pain motivates us to action. If we have a toothache, we call a dentist. When a stomach pain hits us so hard in the middle of the night that we can't stand, we go to the hospital emergency room. We don't know whether it's a ruptured appendix, gall stones, or just a bad stomachache. No matter the reason for our pain, we immediately try to do something about it.

And when we react to our pain, we probably keep ourselves from being hurt any further. If it were a small pain, we might put off doing anything about it, but *big* pains get immediate reaction.

Finally, pain becomes our teacher when God wants to teach us something. So maybe our pain doesn't turn us to our life purpose, nor is it used to strengthen our character, but maybe our pain teaches us an important lesson that we can only learn in our misery. Notice what David said: "My troubles turned out all for the best—they forced me to learn from your textbook" (Ps. 119:71, *THE MESSAGE*).

There are always reasons for pain. You don't hurt unless there is a problem, and our problems can be a classroom that teaches us what God wants us to know.

—————— WRAP-UP ——————

Obviously, there can be many reasons for our pain and we can learn many different things from it. In a mature Christian, pain may build deeper character, build greater faith, or prepare him/her for more productive service. Pain can draw the mature believer into closer intimacy with God. Whatever the reason, pain always has a purpose. Those who are suffering will probably continue in their anguish until they find out what purpose God has for them through their pain.

Five Rewards from Pain

- **Pain forces you to Look** . . . to the Word of God for answers.

- **Pain forces you to Lean** . . . on the arm of God instead of man.

- **Pain forces you to Learn** . . . where you went astray.

- **Pain forces you to Long** . . . for His Presence and healing.

- **Pain forces you to Listen** . . . for changes in God's instructions.[2]

Notes

1. Unknown source.
2. Jamie Wright, Sermon Central. http://www.sermoncentral.com/sermon.asp?SermonID=74483&ContributorID=11041 (accessed April 2006).

4

COPING

YOUR REACTION TO PAIN

I don't accept the maxim "there's no gain without pain,"
physical or emotional. I believe it is possible to develop and grow with
joy rather than grief. However, when the pain comes my way,
I try to get the most growth out of it.

ALEXA MCLAUGHLIN
(FREELANCE EDITOR AND WRITER)[1]

Sometimes you suffer unrelenting pain associated with a disease, or an actual accident. The pain is a real challenge because you've never hurt this badly before. The pain is tense ... unrelenting ... and it is usually unique.

Sometimes the pain is not from the disease itself, but from the side effects caused by the disease. As an illustration, you may get an infection from an open wound, causing inflammation that produces pain; so doctors don't know whether to give you a prescription to treat your actual pathology, or medicine to treat the side effects of your disease.

And then there is a third cause of pain, the side effects from the drug you have been using. As an illustration, I took chemo for my cancer. The doctor told me that my particular type of chemo would creep on the surface of the skin or intestine to attack any cancer cells that may be growing there. My chemo didn't deal with cancer in the blood or cancer growing in an organ. Since I had a malignant tumor that grew on my colon,

I was given chemo to attack any other small cells that might be growing on an intestine like the original cancer. What happened? I broke out in rashes and small scabs all over my chest and arms, and blisters appeared on the soles of my feet. The chemo was attacking initiatory melanoma on my chest that was the result of not wearing a shirt as a boy. Did those small scabs itch? *Absolutely!!* No one knows how deeply you desire to scratch until you begin scratching, and then you fall into a trap of more scratching to suffice the pain. But the more you scratch the more you inflict damage, and ultimately increase the inflammation and pain.

Then there were a few other side effects of my chemo that caused discomfort, i.e., constipation and nausea. But the irritating side effects were worth enduring to rid myself of life-threatening cancer.

A fourth type of pain is mental or emotional anguish. Perhaps you are not able to do the things that you used to do, at least not without great effort and physical drive. You can't roll over on your side in bed, so you lie stationary on your back. Then you get painful bedsores that come from avoiding the pain of rolling over. Then you can't get out of bed without someone pulling you up, and you even walk with pain. You have to think about every step, because you don't naturally walk.

That physical pain causes mental stress and pain. When you can't get out of bed without help, you feel a certain amount of despair and anxiety; you have to call someone to help you, which leads to more anxiety—and frustration. Then a few people who can't help themselves go to a deeper level of pain—anger. Each pain has a different intensity level and each pain has a different frustration level.

Eighteen Reactions to Pain

Sometimes your reaction to pain is more important than the pain itself. Yes, you hurt. And yes, you hate pain—what normal person likes to suffer? But your reaction can help you get through the difficulty.

Once a young bride from the East married during wartime, and her husband was transferred to a U.S. Army base in the desert of California. Living conditions were marginal, the heat was unbearable, the desert constantly blew dust and sand in the house, and her days were boring because her husband was gone most of the time. Their neighbors spoke only Spanish or were Native Americans from the reservation who did not speak English.

The young woman wrote her mother that she was coming home because she couldn't take it anymore. Her mother wrote back simply two lines:

Two men looked through prison bars: One saw mud; the other saw stars.

The woman felt ashamed because of her complaints, and decided she would look to the stars. She made friends with the Indians, learned weaving, pottery-making, and eventually learned everything she could about Indian history and culture. Later in life she became an expert and wrote a book on the area.

First, since suffering is inevitable, don't think you are unusual. Pain is promised to everyone in a finite body; organs will wear out, blood vessels will clog, cells will grow into cancer, and wet clothing on a cold day may produce a head cold. And there are always accidents: we'll break a bone, hyper-extend a finger, fall off a high place, skin our shin, or stub our toe when we get out of bed in the dark night. Job, the man who suffered most, realized pain was inevitable: "Yet man is born to trouble, as the sparks fly upward" (Job 5:7).

Second, don't immediately think that God is punishing you for a sin when something goes wrong in your body. Yes, sometimes pain is punishment, as when God told Eve because of her sin, "I will greatly multiply your sorrow and your conception; in pain you shall bring forth children" (Gen. 3:16). But most of our physical problems come because we live in an imperfect world. Since we don't live in heaven, accidents happen and people hurt. AIDS gets spread through sexual contact, and people suffer.

People do stupid things and wreck their cars, destroy their liver with alcohol, or a mother-to-be smokes cigarettes that endanger the life of her unborn child.

When you immediately hurt, pain protects you by shutting down the body so that you won't face more damage. Nobody thinks when they smash a finger in the door that this pain is good, but pain will make you give immediate attention to the problem. It's more than yelling, "*Y-e-e-e-o-o-o-w-w-w!*"

I read the story of an African leper cooking on an open fire. His meat dropped into the fire, so he reached in, grabbed it and took it out. Because the nerve endings of lepers are damaged and they don't feel pain, they unknowingly do further damage to themselves. The leper who dropped his food in the fire severely burned his hand—second-degree burn. He was scrounging around in red-hot coals not realizing his fingers were being cooked like raw meat. If he had a feeling of pain, he would have jerked his hand out of the fire to prevent further damage. But the leper lost parts of his fingers because of that accident.

For some—probably very few—their suffering is tied to their sin. When the lame man was healed at the Pool of Bethesda, Jesus, who knows all things, realized what destroyed the legs of the lame man. We can only imagine! Perhaps he got drunk and fell in the street and a wagon rolled over his legs. Maybe it was some other sin that destroyed his legs. Anyway, Jesus told him, "Sin no more, lest a worse thing come upon you" (John 5:14). What does this mean? If the man went back to his previous sin, something worse would happen to him than losing the use of his legs.

Third, since there is a divine purpose for pain, learn what God wants to teach you. Remember, God does not send pain to His people; He allows it because He works all things together for good that we might be conformed to the image of His Son (see Rom. 8:28-29). So in between your groans and complaints, squeeze in time to pray. First, ask God to teach you what He wants you to learn about this suffering. Next, look at your pain through God's eyes to see what He sees. Finally, trust God for the results for healing from pain, as well as using you in His kingdom.

Fourth, sometimes you will suffer because you are attacked for your faith. Peter says in 1 Peter 4:16, "Yet if [anyone suffers] as a Christian, let him not be ashamed, but let him glorify God in this matter" (1 Pet. 4:16). Therefore, if you know you are suffering because you are a Christian, there is purpose to your suffering. As it is said so often, it's easy to endure suffering when you have a purpose for your pain, and you have hope that someday your pain will be over.

Commit your soul to God in suffering. Sometimes all you can do is yield yourself to God. Didn't Peter tell us, "Therefore let those who suffer according to the will of God commit their souls [to Him] in doing good, as to a faithful Creator" (1 Pet. 4:19)?

Fifth, remember that most everyone will leave this life in pain. The Bible describes it as "the pains of death" (Acts 2:24; Ps. 116:3). Death is described as "crossing the River Jordan," and most people think Jordan is deep, wide and chilly. This suggests that our pain may be deep and wide because pain will last a long time and pain will chill the soul.

This leads to a sixth realization: you will have more pain (and probably more serious pain) in your old age than in adolescence and young adulthood. Why does God send more pain to senior adults? Maybe it's because our organs are wearing out and our resistance is lower than ever. Why does God build us that way? Because if we were strong and healthy right until our death, we would fight death. If we had no pain right until death, we wouldn't look forward to living with Jesus on the other side of death's door. And if we had no suffering, we couldn't really glorify God in our death.

In the seventh place, remember that Jesus died through suffering; so why should we be exempt from that ordeal? Doesn't the Bible say, "Therefore we were buried with Him through baptism into death, that just as Christ was raised from the dead by the glory of the Father, even so we also should walk in newness of life" (Rom. 6:4)? What does that mean? When Christ was on the cross, dying for us, we were identified with Him because we were positionally placed into Him so that when He died, we died with

Him. So, the way that Jesus left this physical world is the same way that we may leave it—through suffering.

In the eighth place, accept what you cannot change. David was grieving over the fact that his one-year-old baby was sick at the point of death. David had committed adultery then arranged for the death of Bathsheba's husband when she became pregnant. David was told by Nathan the prophet, "You are the man" (2 Sam. 12:7). David's sin against God was responsible for the sickness of his child.

David fasted and prayed seven days for the child to be healed. When David heard the servants talking among themselves, he realized the child was dead. Then David got up from the ground and said, "While the child was alive, I fasted and wept... But now he is dead; why should I fast?" (2 Sam. 12:22-23). David knew that he couldn't raise the child from the dead; it was over. So he accepted what he could not change. He got up, took a bath, and went about his daily duties. What about you? Is you first response to accept what you can't change?

Ninth, don't exaggerate your pain; play it down and pray it up. So what did David do after his child died? "He went into the house of the LORD and worshiped" (2 Sam. 12:20). He ignored his pain and recognized God's will for his life.

Those who exaggerate their pain probably suffer more than those who play it down. If you cringe with pain every time the nurse comes in with a needle, you're probably suffering more. But if you accept the inevitable, you won't feel the pain until the needle pricks your arm, and then probably the pain won't be as severe as those who are yelling over the intrusion of the needle.

Tenth, focus on the good you have left in life, not the bad that was lost. Most people who are in the hospital will get out sometime in life. They may not be as agile when they walk, they may not be able to run a marathon, or they may have lost a limb or some other more severe calamity, but they have their life, and that's good!

So when you get out of the hospital, focus on the good things you have left, look to the future, and expect God to use your life. Notice what David did after his child died: "Then David comforted Bathsheba his wife . . . She bore a son, and he called his name Solomon" (2 Sam. 12:24).

Isn't that a wonderful picture? Even though they lost a child, God gave them another. So when you lose something in life, look forward to what God will give you next. But then there's another thing: Solomon became the wisest man on earth, took over the kingdom from David and ruled in peace. Solomon was God's gift to an otherwise bereaving couple.

Eleventh, people may hurt you, but never retaliate. God can replace grudges with blessings. If your pain comes from a relationship, someone who has done you wrong, or someone who hasn't done anything at all—they snubbed you—what are you going to do? Are you going to curse them, pray evil on them, or retaliate in some way? That's not the Christian answer. What did Jesus say? "Bless them that curse you, and pray for them which despitefully use you" (Luke 6:28).

While you're in the hospital, you look for people to come and bless you with their presence and prayers. But let's reverse the action; you need to pray for those who don't come to the hospital room, or pray for those who come with wrong motives. You become the one who does the blessing, and they become the ones who receive it.

And what happens to you when you become a blessing? You take your mind off your pain, and you even take your mind off of why you are in pain. You think of the other person, and in doing so, you lessen your pain and speed up healing.

If I allow pain to make me bitter,
it blinds me to the truth of what God wants to do in my life.

MARTIN LUTHER

Twelfth, let God do His work in your life. When you pray for God to alleviate pain, remember that you're not living in heaven where there is no pain. You're living on this earth, where pain is a natural reaction to sickness, and there's natural suffering from accidents, and where calamities steal everything from you. Therefore, when you have pain, remember that God loves you and has a plan for your pain. So what should you do? You must seek God's purpose to understand what He is doing in your life.

So you live in a world of pain where you *hurt*! Look beyond your hurt and into the heart of God. Find out what God is trying to do in your life and yield to His purpose.

Remember, you're living on a sinful earth with sinful people who do sinful things—and sometimes they hurt you. Also, you're living on an earth where there are germs, disease, and a worldwide epidemic of AIDS, plus the threat of pandemic bird flu. Just because there are all of these things doesn't mean God has lost control of the world. The opposite is true: while sin is playing out its hand, God is working His perfect plan in the lives of those who love and trust Him.

Thirteenth, remember that Jesus wants to heal your hurting heart. When you hurt in the body, remember that Jesus wants you to be spiritual. Just as He came to earth to compassionately heal those who were sick, in the same way Jesus has compassion on you. He doesn't want to hurt you; He wants to heal you. So seek His healing. Remember, "the prayer of faith shall save the sick" (Jas. 5:15).

Fourteenth, look past your pain with hope for the future. Remember, every flood eventually subsides when the waters go away. In the same way, your pain will eventually go away and you'll feel better. You'll have a wonderful day sometime in the future. But perhaps not all will. If some were to die, remember what Paul said: "For me living is for Christ, and dying is even better" (Phil. 1:21, *TLB*). Paul didn't know if life or death were best: "For I am hard pressed between the two, having a desire to depart and be with Christ, [which is] far better" (Phil. 1:23).

Notice what Job said about the receding flood waters: "If you would prepare your heart, and stretch out your hands toward Him; if iniquity [were] in your hand, [and you] put it far away, and would not let wickedness dwell in your tents; then surely you could lift up your face without spot; yes, you could be steadfast, and not fear; because you would forget [your] misery, and remember [it] as waters [that have] passed away" (Job 11:13-16).

The fifteenth reaction is tied to physical alienation and healing: believe what your pain is telling you. Remember, I told you the story of my broken ribs and how I tried to act as though they did not hurt. That was not a normal reaction, nor was it smart. There are obvious physical causes for pain; believe them and react accordingly.

Remember that pain does more than hurt; it saps energy and stamina from your life. Pain makes you feel irritable, tired, and when you fight pain for a long time, you're exhausted. So, when people do things for you, you may become short-tempered. Your loved ones don't realize what's happening on the inside, so they think you are ungrateful. Then an emotional barrier comes between you and your loved ones; that's a whole new realm of pain to deal with. Learn to accept love and support from your friends and don't create any barriers by your negative reactions.

Sixteenth, learn to relax and get the therapeutic value of rest. It sounds like an oxymoron, but work at relaxing rather than fighting your pain. Rest makes it easier to heal.

Seventeenth, listen to your doctor and let him know as much about your pain as possible. Perhaps he can prescribe an antidote or pain killer. When he does, take your medicine properly and accurately. When he tells you two pills will relieve the pain, don't take four, six or eight. The side effects may be worse than its intended cure.

When your doctor gives you some exercises to help improve muscle strength to relieve pain, try to do what he has instructed. Exercise produces endorphins, which are natural chemicals produced by the body to reduce pain.

Eighteenth, set small goals for yourself. When I was lying flat on my back and couldn't turn over, I'd turn a quarter of the way and stick a pillow behind my back, thus relieving some of the pain. I did that until I was able to turn on my side. The doctor told me to walk down the hospital hallway to the nurses' station, but I could barely make it to the door. Yet each time I walked, I increased the distance by a little until I could do it without help.

When I returned to teaching my classes at Liberty University, I could barely walk from my car to the classroom, then I sat down to teach. Before long, I was able to walk from my office to my classroom, and each day I practiced standing for short periods of time as I taught my class. Eventually, I was able to stand during the entire lecture.

Note

1. Alexa McLaughlin. http://en.thinkexist.com/quotations/pain/10.html (accessed June 2006).

Section Two

THE WORST THING THAT COULD HAPPEN

Pain is like a worn-out part on your car. You hear a strange noise and ignore it because your car keeps running. And just as a worn part steals a little power, so too little pains slow you down or you lose a little distance on your golf drive. Then your car lurches and sputters—it's like a pain that tosses you into bed for a day. Finally, the worn part breaks and your car chugs to a halt. You're stranded beside the road, or you're laid up in a hospital bed. Now you hurt. Your pain is so bad you cry out, "Why me . . . why this . . . why now?"

Chapter 5 describes the helplessness you feel when pain completely debilitates you. Chapter 6 deals with your fears that only accentuate your pain so that you become bitter. Chapter 7 describes how you cry out from the bottom of a hole in anguish. Chapter 8 describes bitterness that makes you turn against everything and everyone. Chapter 9 describes how the next step downward is anguish when you give up.

If the negative emotions of this section don't grab you, rejoice. If they do, go quickly to the next section because there's hope in your darkest hour.

5

HELPLESSNESS

A HOSPITAL MAKES YOU FEEL
ABSOLUTELY HELPLESS

If pain was not followed by pleasure, who could forbear it?
ANONYMOUS[1]

The hospital: a place where you are absolutely necessary as the intended target for doctors and nurses and the object of millions of dollars of miraculous machinery designed to make you well. But in an opposite viewpoint: a hospital is a place where you feel absolutely unnecessary because your destiny is taken out of your hands. A hospital makes you feel absolutely helpless.

Think of all the things done for you while a patient in a hospital. You eat when the server brings your tray. You hold up your arm for a blood sample when the nurse arrives with the needle. You swallow a pill not knowing its intended purpose, and lie there with nothing to do. Even visitors and friends pop in according to their schedule, not when you need them. A nurse wakes you up in the morning to take your temperature, even when you're sound asleep and you don't want to wake up. And then to top if all off, the nurse turns out the light at night for you to go to sleep when you're not sleepy.

So what do you do when all this commotion goes on all around you? Nothing but comply with every request.

And what about outside the hospital? You have cancer and you're taking chemotherapy or radiation treatments. If the medication is intrusive, you lose your hair, suffer diarrhea, tolerate an unbearable itch, or need a nap two or three times a day because the chemo weakens you.

You're supposed to be recuperating and getting well. But what happens to those loved ones and friends around you? Instead of making you feel more valuable to the human race, they inadvertently and ignorantly push you into the downward cycle of helplessness. They say, "I'll cut the grass for you," or "Save the dishes; I'll do them." Sometimes our friends run our errands, get the car lubricated; some may even write thank-you notes for flowers and expressions of sympathy.

And to increase our dependence, they say, "Move in with us until you feel better," or the reverse, "I'm going to come and stay a few days so I can tend to things around the house."

So what has happened? In the process of helping you over your sickness and pain, they inadvertently make you helpless.

When you lose your independence, you feel helpless. And going a step further, when you give up your responsibility to the many tasks in your life, you feel helpless. Then our helplessness gives us an empty pain, sometimes as hurtful as our physical pain.

The Theology of the To-Do List

Pity the sick person who has no to-do list. Why is that bad? Because if you have no to-do list, you're not needed. As a result, you usually feel like there's no reason or purpose to go on living.

A to-do list is a wonderful intrusive tool that communicates great spiritual benefits. A to-do list makes us focus on the future and teaches us hope, because we must show up sometime in the future to perform certain duties on our list. Since hope is foundational for healing, then a to-do list is a tool of hope.

We get our *identity* from a to-do list. Usually, the items on our to-do list are tasks that only we can do. You go to pick out paint for the recreation room, because you're the only one who knows which color will best match the furniture. You have to pick up batteries, because no one knows what size of cavity where the batteries fit. We are the only ones to explain to the teacher why Johnny needs two days off from school. And when we pick up orange juice, anti-dandruff shampoo and nose drops, we're the only ones who know the exact brand we like. So our to-do list makes us human, and when you examine your to-do list carefully, it dictates what only you can do—so you're necessary to life.

Don't forget about happiness. A to-do list gives us a sense of accomplishment and that gives us satisfaction. You're doing what your to-do list tells you is necessary to stay alive and gain a modicum of meaning to the eternal riddle: "Why am I here?"

Our life is restored when the paint we select for the recreation room fits perfectly with our color scheme. And doesn't everyone want to be perfect?

Let's take a moment to look at the obvious pendulum that we have created. Clearly, we need someone to help us when we're sick. When my stomach muscles were cut by a 15-inch incision, I needed my wife to pull me up in the bed so I could at least sit up to eat. I even needed her help to get out of the bed to get to the bathroom. Sick people need a lot of help, and without it, perhaps they won't get well. But remember that the help we give them may be the two-edged sword that takes away their dignity.

If I had to choose whether to take the help of others or remain sick in the bed, I obviously would choose the loss of control over my life.

Pain blocks out what you're thinking. Pain, like an enemy, steals into your mind with a sponge to erase vital thought patterns. You forget the things that make you happy, and your confidence is eradicated. Pain makes you forget your warm relationships with friends and the places you like to eat, or even the enjoyment of hiking a country trail or the thrill of attainment you get from completing an exercise routine.

Pain is the virus that slips into the computer of your mind to plant awful messages on your hard drive. Will I be able to go back to work? Will I ever play golf again? Will I lose my job? How can I pay for the expensive hospital bills? Will someone else take my place?

Remember, sometimes to go forward up the mountain, you have to dip through a valley or two. So to get well, you have to take yourself out of the loop, and give up the control of your life to someone else. The byproduct of that choice is helplessness.

And there is something else. Treatment, medicine and surgery make every action tenuous and complicated. We don't like surgery, but we know it is the path to healing. We don't like the medicine, but we know it's the tool to make us well.

While you're in pain, you have to make constant choices. You have to walk a delicate balance between giving up control and taking control of your life. It's a delicate balance between mastery and helplessness.

It's a terrible task to lie in a bed of pain and not be able to do anything about it. You want to do something to feel better, but you abide by the hospital schedule. The hospital personnel look upon you as a business object—a patient. They seem to forget that you're still a person; the problem is that you just have a malfunction of the body.

What is health? So often we define health as not being sick, or we say that "health is the absence of pain or disease." But is health just the opposite of sickness? Is health living our life in neutral? Automatic transmissions in our automobiles have drive and reverse, between them is neutral. When we press the accelerator, the motor roars, but the car doesn't move. The car is in neutral! Is health like neutral on the gear shift? The answer is no!

We need to define health in light of being able to do what we want to do. Health is both the desire and the ability to do our work. Health is the capacity to enjoy the things in life that make life meaningful. Health is a lot more than just getting over a fever or getting our strength back. Health is a positive capacity to do all that God has intended us to do.

When I came home from the hospital, the pain subsided and I just moped around the house for several days. I was getting my physical health back, but something was desperately wrong! My desire to do things was gone, I didn't have the emotional drive to do anything, and I had lost my appetite for work.

I sat at my desk to work on a chapter of a book, and got up a few moments later because I couldn't concentrate. It wasn't writer's block. To have a block suggests that when you are moving forward, something stops your action. The problem was inertia—I wasn't moving at all. I was getting my physical health back, but my stamina for work was gone.

I met God in the morning for prayer, but my sharp-edge of anticipation was gone from intercession. I read the Bible, but I didn't seem to care if I received a message from God or not. I was getting physically healthy, but not mentally. So I wasn't healthy!

A four-day golf tournament came on television. With the satellite dish on my television set, I was able to watch from nine in the morning till dark each day. I sat there silently like a zombie, staring at the television set for 10 hours a day. Do you see the problem I had? Do you see the connection between hopelessness and poor health? I was not healthy because I had no desire to do anything, even when I had the free time to spring into action. Helplessness is the opposite of health.

So when we think of the helpless person suffering pain, let's think in terms of the future and what they can do. Let's try to get them to imagine themselves in a situation where they are being productive and are needed in life. Remember, health is more than a bodily function; health is the strength of mind and purpose of heart to be excited about what God wants you to do.

So let's be careful around people who are sick or suffering pain. Let's make sure that we don't immobilize both their body and their spirit. When we motivate a person to live and compete, we are producing health. When we engender a spirit of conquest, we have given them perhaps better medicine than a medical prescription, or better healing than any hospital treatment.

Remember, doctors do not heal us; they only cut away malignancy, or they remove a tumor, or they give us medicine to counteract germs, or they prescribe exercise to make us healthy. No, a doctor doesn't heal; the body heals itself.

This wonderful mechanism called the human body has the God-given strength to heal itself when we suffer from germs, viruses, diseases or injury. The doctors prescribe medicine that may cause an interruption, cessation or removal of our pathology. They may begin the healing process by surgery, but in the end, the body heals itself.

So when we are healed, many different kinds of changes take place in the body. But also remember that our emotions play a vital role in healing the body. When we are happy with an aggressive desire to get well, we are much more likely to be healed than if we are discouraged, pessimistic or have given up in the process.

What Is Helplessness?

- A fear that we will not be normal again

- Loneliness of being left alone with nothing to do

- A realization that we are completely inadequate.

- A realization that our body has something wrong, and a fear that we won't get better

- A lack of self-respect because we're in a hospital gown with our backside protruding, where nothing is private, and all our personal dignities are exposed

---

There's another thing about pain. Remember, pain increases in intensity when you do nothing but think about it all day long. At the same time, medical research has shown that when the patient's thinking is distracted away from his pain, he does not suffer as much. We can learn two lessons: First, the more your pain causes helplessness and frustration, the more you will think about your pain and the more you will suffer. That truth leads to a second practical consideration: Distraction reduces pain. You are beginning to get healthy when you think about life after your sickness, or you plan where you will eat after the hospital diet is over, or when you see yourself back on the golf course. The more you think about living for God and doing His will, the less you will focus on your pain; therefore, the less you will suffer.

The businessman in the hospital completely forgets about his pain when his administrative assistant brings a report that must be done. Because the sick executive has a report that must be completed—and only he can do it—the thought of pain is diverted while the businessman is lost in his world of work.

So what does that tell us? Maybe just aimlessly lying in a hospital bed is not the best way to full recovery. Maybe we should be doing something up to the edge of our desire, rather than being a passive vegetable waiting for the nurse to come into our room to take another blood sample.

People think that distraction of thoughts is the best way to deal with pain. Think about it: Sometimes when you take aspirin or another pain reliever, the pain doesn't go away because you continue to focus on what is making you hurt. However, when you give full attention to some diversionary project, you don't think about pain; hence, you don't suffer as deeply.

———————— WRAP-UP ————————

Helplessness is despair, but wholeness comes when you feel needed by your friends, or you feel loved by your family, or you're working to fulfill your dreams.

One of the best cures for helplessness is helping others. In other words, the best way to get rid of your feeling of helplessness is to help somebody else who suffers from the finality of helplessness.

So think of Christian service and what you can do in the church. Think of other people up and down the hospital corridor whom you can help. Think of a phone call to encourage someone or a letter to support a struggling college student. You'll probably forget about your pain as you try to help other people get through their pain, and you'll lose your feeling of helplessness when you help someone who is helpless.

Note

1. Quote from anonymous source.

6

FEAR

FEAR MAKES SUFFERING
MORE PAINFUL

*We're not necessarily doubting that God will do the best for us;
we are wondering how painful the best will turn out to be.*

C. S. LEWIS[1]

The greatest barrier to your recovery is fear. Extreme pain scares you to death. Your fear grabs your mind and won't let you think about anything but your pain. Fear seizes your heart and won't let you dream of recovery. Fear imprisons your will, forcing you to give up.

When fear makes you surrender to pain, then the pain intensifies.

As I walk through the hospital, I see all the healing machines at the nurses' station; my first reaction is to marvel at the millions of dollars they've spent to help people get well. Also, I marvel at all the miraculous drugs that seemingly produce supernatural healing. Yet all our curing machines and wonder drugs have not banished the greatest villain of all—fear.

What happens when you are afraid? Probably your first reaction is physical. Muscles tighten, eyes dilate, blood pressure goes up, and your mouth gets dry. And that's just the body. What about the mind? You don't think rationally; you take heroin, opium, morphine and you're not afraid of becoming an addict;

you're afraid of pain. As a matter of fact, your mind gets confused and you can't think rationally at all.

Remember that fear doesn't make us optimistic because there's no hope in fear. If anything, fear steals all hope. When fear feeds on itself, it produces dread. That means you get more scared the more pain you feel, and you think about dying. You become more scared that the pain will intensify and kill you. You're frightened you'll leave your spouse and children behind without proper care. Then your breathing either races or it does the reverse and you begin gasping for breath because you can't breathe.

Minimizing Fear

Let's talk realistically about my fears. I hate hypodermic needles of all kinds. When I was going through my chemo treatment, every three weeks I went in for an examination and they took a sample of blood. That involved sticking a needle in a vein in my left arm. When I looked at the needle, everything wrong happened in my head. I felt pain and wanted to yell, "Ouch," even before they stuck me with the needle. I did what every brave man does: I looked the other direction. Then the nurse said, "Stick," and I felt a small prick in my arm and the needle was in. Fear of needle pain is a hundred times greater than the actual pain that a small prick produces. But when I don't see it coming, it doesn't hurt as much.

Why do I feel more pain in anticipation than in reality? Fear.

Let's use another illustration. When the dentist begins to grind in an empty cavity of a tooth, I stiffen like a board. Every muscle in my body is taut, my heart races, and I am absolutely sure that the dentist will hit a nerve so that I'll scream bloody murder. I know in my head that the attendant has given me novocaine, but I fearfully dread the grinding drill. After the grinding starts, I can feel vibration in the bones of my head, but it doesn't hurt nearly as much as I expected. Why such a negative reaction to a dental procedure? Fear.

There is a third illustration to prove my point. Think of the diabetics who constantly have to plunge a needle into their body.

With time, it becomes ordinary and routine. A needle stick becomes nothing. Why? Because there is no fear.

When you're in the hospital, they may give you morphine to relieve your pain. Doctors say that the more confidence patients have in morphine, the more it will do to reduce pain. As a matter of research, a patient's confidence will actually help block more pain signals to the brain than the morphine-medicine itself. What does that say to you? Our fears make us hurt a lot more than we actually do. And our confidence reduces our pain—we don't hurt as much as we should.

Many who are suffering pain feel that God has abandoned them. They cry out in prayer, and feel their words bounce off the ceiling. This produces fear that the worst will happen to them.

But there is a step further: fear eats away your assurance. When you're scared to death and try to pray, sometimes it doesn't work. Why? Because your fears convince you that God will not hear you, even before you pray. And if you don't have faith in prayer, you can't pray in faith for God to heal you (see Jas. 5:15).

Let's Get Rid of Fear

A lot of people think that when you know what's happening to you, it will take away your fear. Maybe! So people may think that when you understand the role of therapy and what you have to do to get well, it will take away fear. Perhaps!

You may have a disease in your body like cancer, and it causes pain and death. But you also may have a disease in your heart called fear, and it too causes death—spiritual death. And with the dread of death comes pain—spiritual pain.

Remember, we said that pain shouts to us in our suffering. Why? Because pain is the body's way to get our attention so that we will do something about our problem. So what happens? You begin listening to your pain and because it speaks so loudly you don't think straight. Your suffering is so acute that you break out in a sweat. You fear that the medicine is not working. You fear that you will not get well. You sometimes even fear that you will die. And when you hurt so badly, you fear that you won't die.

Who was it in the Bible who said, "Perfect love casts out fear" (1 John 4:18)? So it's love that will get rid of your fears. It's not your knowledge of medicine, or therapy, or even the confidence in your doctor that will drive away fear. It's your confidence in God. You have to remember that God has a purpose for your suffering, and the key thing is not your suffering but your reaction to pain. You can choose to learn what God wants you to know from pain, and get stronger spiritually. You can be transformed by pain.

So what does perfect love have to do with fear? When we know that God loves us and that He has a plan for our life, then we entrust everything to Him. We welcome His love and grace. We love Him back. That takes away fear.

There are a lot of things that will cut fear out of your life, like the doctor cuts away malignant cancer. We've already said that prayer is one of those things that takes away fear. (See chapter 12 on faith healing to understand more deeply how to pray for those who are sick).

Fellowship with our Christian friends is also necessary. When they come to see you, what happens? You reestablish a link to their life and they remind you who they are, and the good times the two of you have had in the past (see chapter 13).

Memory can be a good thing because it tells us the truth— where we've been and what we were. If we have been happy in life and if God has used us, then it's likely that God will use our memory to give us hope in the future.

Memory can become a bad thing—when we are controlled by fear. When we remember our past good times, but we let our fear convince us they will never return, it's then that our pain intensifies.

Bible reading is good because it gets our focus off our suffering when we begin to read about God, think about God, and focus our attention on God. After all, isn't He the only One who can help us?

As I said earlier, I have a trilogy of questions I often ask when I get in trouble: "Why me? Why now? Why this?"

A few years ago I was rushing from our church service to attend another meeting at another church, and at the top of the hill leading away from our church, my front tire blew out. Obviously, I complained, "Why me? Why now? Why this?" I jumped out of the car, took off my coat, rolled up my sleeves, and hurriedly began emptying my trunk of the jack, lever, and spare tire. Even though it was a steamy hot day, I was not yet burning in physical pain. My pain was mental; I was worried because I was late, even though I knew it really didn't matter. My part in the program could be shifted to a later time. My greatest mental pain was not living up to the expectation of arriving everywhere on time.

In the middle of all my frustration, I backed away from the tire, went over to stand in the shade, and surveyed the situation. I thought about what I had to do, how unnecessary I was to the church program, and what would happen if I didn't show up. Then it dawned on me: I didn't have to show up. And then another thing dawned on me: I didn't have to show up on time. In that moment, I yielded the entire circumstances to God.

The story has a pleasant ending. About the time I surrendered my frustration to God, along came a young father of two kids in an old classic pickup truck that had a beautiful shiny baby-blue gloss paint job. Obviously, this young father loved working on his truck. All he had on were blue jeans; no shirt, no shoes. He jumped out of his truck and yelled, "Let me do that for you, Sir."

Gladly I allowed him to do it. I didn't want to get hot or sweaty, so I just watched with amazement at his joy in changing a tire. I knew he wanted money so when he was finished I gave him a $20 bill. And more than that, I talked to him about getting those two children in Sunday school and his obligation to be the father that God would have him be.

Let's Keep Some Fears

We ought to be grateful for fear, for our fears sometimes keep us from doing dangerous things—things that might destroy us. Think of the things that frighten you. The little boy is afraid to dive off the high diving board. Maybe that's good fear because he doesn't know how to dive into the water without being hurt. The young man is scared by a snake in the path, and that's good because it keeps him from being poisoned. The teenager is afraid to smoke a joint, and his fear keeps him from becoming an addict. Fear, like pain, serves as a warning to keep us from further harm.

Should we try to get rid of people's fears? Absolutely not! For when people have no fear, they are open to all types of danger.

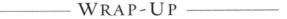

WRAP-UP

In this chapter I have tried to tell you how to deal with your fear, even get rid of your fears. But there is a fear that you ought to fear the most. It is a fear of not pleasing God; it is the fear of disobeying the commandants of God. And didn't Jesus tell us, "Don't be afraid of those who want to kill you. They can only kill your body; they cannot touch your soul. Fear only God, who can destroy both soul and body in hell" (Matt. 10:28, *NLT*)?

Note

1. C. S. Lewis, British scholar and novelist, 1898-1963. http://en.thinkexist.com/quotes/c.s._lewis/2.html (accessed March 2006).

7

CRYING OUT

THE CONSTANT TEMPTATION
TO GIVE UP

What we do not see, what most of us never suspect of existing,
is the silent but irresistible power which comes to the rescue of those
who fight on in the face of discouragement.

NAPOLEON HILL[1]

Pain is a storm, and when you're caught in a life-threatening storm, you lose all sense of balance, comfort and safety. When life becomes so rough like the waves of the storm that threaten to drown you, realize that God is the Creator of everything, including storms.

What is it about a storm that scares us? Are we afraid of drowning, so we panic and cry for help? Are we afraid of getting hit by flying objects? No, probably death is not our greatest concern in the storm. It's something else!

Storms mess everything up. Storms destroy our houses, crash trees into our cars, and when the storm rips the roof off our house, the rain destroys everything that is precious to us. Isn't that what we are afraid of in the storm—losing our possessions?

Sometimes when things go easy, we don't cry out to God. When we have money left over from our paycheck, and our children do well in the school play, and we shoot the best golf score of our life, we don't cry out to God with either praise or a plea for help. We enjoy our possessions and accomplishments, then go on our merry way.

Have you ever thought that God sends us into the storm, dropping us in the middle of a squall of howling winds and breaking waves so that we have no other option but to cry out, "Lord, save me"?

There's a story in the Bible of Jesus coming to the disciples in a storm, walking on the water. That story is a parallel to some of us who have gone through life-threatening storms: a cancer storm, a surgery storm, a storm of physical pain. Let's apply some of the lessons of Jesus coming to the disciples in a storm on the Sea of Galilee to our going through a medical storm.

First, Jesus knows everything, so He knew that a storm was coming. And what does He do? "Jesus made His disciples get into the boat and go before Him to the other side" (Matt. 14:22). He sent His disciples into a storm. Has it ever occurred to you that Jesus knows about the disease in our bodies long before doctors diagnose it? Has it ever occurred to you that Jesus sends the storms of surgery into your life? Just as sin-storms terrorize us, so too does an imminent cancer surgery.

Jesus could have had the disciples walk around the lake on dry land because He knew the storm was coming. Also Jesus could have had the disciples stay on the safety of the shore because He knew the storm was coming. Why did He send them into the teeth of the storm? Because only in difficulties could they learn the best lesson of all. And what is that lesson? That Jesus is Immanuel—"God with Us."

When you are incapacitated in a hospital bed, it's hard to grasp that God is with you. But when you realize that there are no other alternatives, then you search for Immanuel.

The disciples knew that Jesus walked with them down the sunny paths of Galilee, but they needed to know that He also could walk with them through the storms on the Sea of Galilee.

Second, when they were in the storms, Jesus was interceding for them: "When He had sent the multitudes away, He went up on the mountain by Himself to pray" (Matt. 14:23). And what do you think He was praying? Since He sent His disciples into the storm, He probably was praying for their safety, for their protection, for them to learn the lesson He wanted to teach.

Has it ever occurred to you that God put you into a hospital bed for physical recovery and for spiritual growth? God wants to teach us lessons through our health problems.

There is a third principle we can learn. Even though the disciples were crying out in the blackness of the storm, Jesus on the shore knew their condition. Why? "He saw them straining at rowing, for the wind was against them" (Mark 6:48). How could Jesus see them when He was miles away? It was in the middle of the night! Because He's God. Jesus is omniscient—He knows everything. So, when you are struggling in a bed of pain, Jesus knows the intensity of your pain even before you cry out to Him—so you don't need to tell Him how much you hurt; He already knows.

The fourth thing is that Jesus came to His disciples in the storm: "He came to them, walking on the sea" (Mark 6:48). So when you cry in the middle of the night, the Lord will come to you, if you have spiritual perception to recognize His presence.

The fifth thing is that the Lord wants us to cry out to Him. Notice a strange thing Jesus did when He came walking to His disciples upon the water: "He came to them, walking on the sea, and would have passed them by" (Mark 6:48). Why do you think He would have passed them by? Notice the wrong perception by the disciples: "They were troubled, saying, 'It is a ghost!' and they cried out for fear" (Matt. 14:26). Isn't it true that when you're scared, you don't recognize Jesus when He is near?

Many on the bed of pain have wrong perceptions of Jesus. They pray in the wrong way and they pray for the wrong thing, because they don't understand what God is doing in their life. When the disciples thought Jesus was a ghost, He immediately spoke to them, "Be of good cheer! It is I; do not be afraid" (Matt. 14:27). Did you see the last part of this verse? *Do not be afraid.* That's what God wants you to learn in your pain: *fear not.*

So you can do something in your hospital bed besides pray desperately, "Help me!" You can take an act of faith that recognizes that (1) Jesus is concerned about your pain; (2) He has a plan and purpose for your pain; and (3) you can trust rather than be afraid in your suffering.

And in another storm, at another place, the disciples came asking Jesus, "Teacher, do You not care that we are perishing?" (Mark 4:38). Are those your words? Are you asking God if He cares about your pain? Then you must exercise faith and recognize that God does care what happens to you. He will come to the exact place where you do not want to be—He will come to your bed of sickness. He may not take away your pain immediately, or He may never take away your pain, but He will be with you. The message of comfort is that Jesus indwells you. Isn't that Christianity? "Christ in you, the hope of glory" (Col. 1:27). So Jesus wants to come to you as you are—in pain—to sit upon the throne of your life and be the Lord of your life. He wants to transform you to be like Himself.

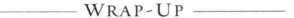

WRAP-UP

Notice that when Jesus "got into the boat, the wind ceased" (Matt. 14:32). When Jesus comes to your bed of pain, He may not take away your pain, but He can stop the storm in your heart. He can give you peace in your suffering, and He can give you peace about what is going to happen in your life. Can you imagine the violent waves crashing on the boat, then suddenly a calm surface on the lake? Think what will happen when the wind quits howling, and the waves no longer threaten, and everything is calm, and the moon comes out from behind the clouds. That's what Jesus wants to do with your heart.

He may not take away your pain, but He wants to give you peace in the midst of your storm.

Note

1. Napoleon Hill, *Creative Quotations*, "discouragement." http://www.quotesandsayings.com/finquoteframes.htm (accessed June 2006).

8

BITTERNESS

WHEN PAIN TURNS YOU AGAINST
EVERYTHING AND EVERYONE

*Time had laid its healing hand upon the wound
when we can look back at the pain we once fainted under,
and no bitterness or despair arises in our heart.*

JEROME K. JEROME (1859-1927)[1]

When Jerry Falwell and I first began Liberty University, we had a young married student, 19 years old, who was among the first students to enroll in our new college. He was energetic to the core, and enthusiastic to the extreme. He would sit on the front row in church and wave his big Bible in the air and shout loudly, "AMEN!" He showed up for every church service through the week, also for every opportunity to serve Christ in the community.

This young student got a part-time delivery job working for a trucking firm. One day as he jumped out of the truck to the ground, he slipped and fractured a leg. There were complications, so he spent two days in the hospital, then came home and couldn't work for two weeks.

We told him not to worry about his schoolwork, and his classmates gave him the lecture notes and kept him up to date with his classes. The church took up a financial offering to cover his hospital bills and salary needs.

Within the next two weeks, this exuberant follower of Jesus Christ became bitter. At times he blamed God for the accident even though everyone told him it was just an accident. As he sat home with his leg in a huge plaster cast, he tried to get around the house on crutches. He first had doubts about his call to ministry. The young student said to himself, "If God called me to prepare for the ministry, why did He allow this accident?"

I tried to tell him, "All things work together for good" (Rom. 8:28), but that consolation didn't really help him. Then I tried to remind him that accidents happen. I tried to explain that in an imperfect world things break, tires blow out, we slip on ice and break a leg; and I tried to explain to him that God did not break his leg, and there was nothing that determined all of life's breaks, accidents and mishaps. These are just the natural results of living in an imperfect world. Still, my arguments didn't reach him.

The young man became extremely bitter and angry. Our dean of men tried to help him in many ways, such as driving him wherever he needed to go, picking him up for church, and bringing his missed assignments to his apartment. But the young man turned on the dean and complained about the good things done for him.

Next, he developed a seed of bitterness toward his wife. Nothing she did for him pleased him. The soup was too hot, she was slow in getting him a heating pad, the house was dirty and cluttered, and she played the television too loud.

Then he became bitter toward God. He criticized, "God knows I want to serve Him; why did He allow my leg to get broken? And since God is a sovereign God, why didn't He heal me?"

What does bitterness look like? It looks like hurting people, wounded people, offended people, or those who just plain suffer.

Bitterness is a choice. When we go through deep suffering, we can choose to trust in God and be happy in the Lord, even though we suffer. Or we can choose to be bitter and compound our suffering. It is said that the difference between bitter and better is one letter.

When people are bitter, they are angry and they usually spew out their hatred towards a doctor who has mistreated them, a friend who has neglected them, or a family member who has ignored them. The bitter person is on a constant roller-coaster ride between his anger and a deep desire to overcome his suffering. The trouble is that with each outburst and expression of bitterness, like a descending spiral, the bitterness plunges deeper and deeper into the soul.

THE POWER OF I
The difference between bitter and better is the letter "i."
I can choose how to react.

To the bitter person, life is rotten and meaningless. They are disillusioned and have no hope in the future. They believe that nothing ever could or would change their circumstances. So, the bitter person has no purpose in life, no meaningful living, and in essence, they have no hope.

Kurt Cobain, lead singer with *Nirvana*, committed suicide, and many of his followers asked why. Kurt Cobain had it all: a voice admired by the world, dedicated fans who bought his albums, a wife and 19-month-old daughter, plus all the money to do anything he wanted to do.

Underneath the opulent lifestyle, Kurt Cobain had a hideous outlook on life that determined his destiny. He was a professed humanist, one that believes that all reality resides within the human person. They reject God and God's wonderful plan for their life. Kurt Cobain was also a nihilist who believed there was no God, no purpose in life, and no meaning to everything about him.

Kurt Cobain pioneered grunge rock with all of its filthiness. At the height of his career, he was the center of his own universe. But when his world was meaningless, he committed suicide.

Belief in God demands that you live above your petty complaints. Your purpose should be to live beyond your human constraints. You must live for God, and no matter what happens, you must believe that the Living God has a wonderful plan for your life.

Jesus calls Satan "the father of lies" (John 8:44). And so what happens? Satan will lie to the person in pain, telling him it's God's fault. If that doesn't work, Satan will lie to the suffering person, telling him the doctors didn't do it right, or the nurses have neglected him. If that doesn't work, Satan lies about friends and family, telling the sufferer that it's their fault, they've neglected you, or they just don't care.

The bitter person has been self-deceived. And the problem with self-deception is that people don't realize how much damage we can do to ourselves. And some have deceived themselves so long that they have difficulty believing anything. Bitterness becomes a way of life.

That means that the bitter person is in bondage or addiction to his bitter approach to life. So, how can the bitter person begin to break his bondage?

First, the bitter person should make sure he is not being controlled by Satan. Remember, "As the serpent deceived Eve by his craftiness, so your minds may be corrupted from the simplicity that is in Christ" (2 Cor. 11:3). Satan will poison our thinking so that we become bitter. So, we must turn to Jesus who said, "And you shall know the truth, and the truth shall make you free" (John 8:32). The positive truths of Scripture can wash away bitterness.

So what must the bitter person do? He must pray, "I acknowledge my bitterness and I want help from God to overcome it."

At times, a bitter person has a real gripe. Perhaps he was injured in an automobile accident, or perhaps a prescription had a side effect that caused permanent physical or mental damage. Even beyond that, perhaps friends or family have blamed the accident and suffering on the patient; he did something stupid so he's now suffering.

What's the second thing a bitter person must do? He must learn to forgive others. Paul said that we must learn forgiveness so that we don't fall into the snare of Satan: "If you forgive anyone, I also forgive him. And what I have forgiven—if there was anything to forgive—I have forgiven in the sight of Christ for your sake, in order that Satan might not outwit us. For we are not unaware of his schemes" (2 Cor. 2:10-11, *NIV*).

Third, the bitter person must list the names of those people he needs to forgive, and actually pray the prayer of forgiveness: "I forgive _____ and pray God's blessing upon that person." As you forgive others, you experience God's forgiveness in your life.

Forgiveness is a choice, just like bitterness is a choice. Because God requires us to forgive others, it's something we can do.

But often we refuse to forgive "those who sin against us." Our bitter choice focuses our hatred on the individual. Our natural inclination is to seek revenge or to retaliate. We rationalize that since we suffer, we're going to make them suffer. When we can't hit them with our fist, we lash out with our tongues to embarrass, humiliate or just plain hurt them. The problem is that when we don't want to let them off the hook, it means they still have their "hook" in our soul.

We don't forgive others for their sake; we forgive them for our sake. And when we pray and seek true forgiveness, we begin to break the bondage of bitterness that addicts our soul.

If you want to see bitterness, look at Job. He cursed the day he was born. Notice his prayer: "Then Job broke the silence. He spoke up and cursed his fate: 'Obliterate the day I was born. Blank out the night I was conceived! Let it be a black hole in space. May God above forget it ever happened. Erase it from the books! May the day of my birth be buried in deep darkness, shrouded by the fog, swallowed by the night. And the night of my conception—the devil take it! Rip the date off the calendar, delete it from the almanac. Oh, turn that night into pure nothingness—no sounds of pleasure from that night, ever! May those who are good at cursing, curse that day. Unleash the sea beast, Leviathan, on it. May its morning stars turn to black cinders, waiting for a daylight that never comes, never once seeing the first light of dawn'" (Job 3:1-9, *THE MESSAGE*).

Did you hear Job spewing out bitterness? Obviously, he's not praising God, nor is he submitting to God's plan for his life. Even though Job bitterly complains, he never curses God—even though he does curse the day he was born. Even though Job is bitter, he's not blaming anyone else for his problems, nor is he blaming God. Job is just bitter and wished he hadn't been born.

Usually when someone curses another, it's in view of harming them now or in the future—a person curses someone to hell. However, Job bitterly looked in the rearview mirror. Can we learn a lesson from this? Yes! We can't change the past. Even though Job cursed the day he was born, his birth was a fact.

There is a movie called *Back to the Future*, whereby a young man went back and changed the events of his present life. But we can't do that! Changing our past only happens in fictitious stories. We are who we are, we are where we are, and we must accept it. We must put our hope in God and live today within the plan of God.

The bitter person is sometimes afraid that he's going to die, and in the next breath, he's afraid he won't die—many bitter people have a death wish. That wasn't Job's problem. Remember that his wife told him, "Curse God and die!" (Job 2:9). He didn't give into that temptation. Job had hope throughout his suffering and he looked to God, prayed to God, and focused his thoughts on the Almighty.

But Job harbored bitterness in his heart. He struggled between self-pity and an inner realization that God existed. Job knew God was sovereign. He constantly begged for God to come and remove him from his pain, or he wanted to debate with God, asking, "Why am I suffering?"

The bitter person has usually resigned himself to his sufferings and has no hope for a better day in the future. No dreams! No future life! There is nothing to do but complain.

The young man described at the beginning of this chapter had great dreams of serving God, and that vision of service was buoyed by his enthusiasm and determination. Yet, when he met his first major obstacle in life—a fractured leg—he couldn't accept its reality. He felt school was over, his dreams were crushed, and there was no use struggling against what he perceived as the inevitable.

Sometimes bitter people have to go back to the point in their life when they gave up. They need to start again from that point. When they have been traveling down the road of bitterness too long, it's difficult to turn around and go back to the fork where they got off track. But nevertheless they must return to the fork and choose God's will. They must submit themselves to God's plan for their life.

Yes, they may suffer, but in God's will they can suffer triumphantly. Yes, they hurt, but in God's economy they can worship God and can make their hospital room a sanctuary. God can come to minister to them in their hour of anguish and help them get through it.

───────── WRAP-UP ─────────

It's possible to turn human defeats into divine victories. Sometimes when pain defeats us, it crushes our selfish ego and stomps on the fleshly yearnings. In defeat, we can come to the end of ourselves and finally yield our life to God. So where does the bitter person have to go? He has to go back to the place where the seed of his root of bitterness was planted. He has to dig up that seed and get forgiveness from God. He must plant a new seed: a seed of obedience, praise and yieldedness.

So bitterness is a choice; therefore, choose not to be bitter, but rather choose to receive the blessing of God.

Note

1. Jerome K. Jerome, *"Idle thought of an Idle Fellow," The Quotations Page.* http://www. quotationspage.com/myquotations.php (accessed March 2006).

9

ANGUISH

THE AGONY OF THOSE IN THE PRISON OF SUFFERING

Character cannot be developed in ease and quiet.
Only through experience of trial and suffering can the soul be
strengthened, ambition inspired, and success achieved.

HELEN KELLER (1880-1968)[1]

Pain is more than feeling bad; it's your conqueror. Pain is the jailer who takes over your life to govern every move that you make. The worst thing about pain is that you lose your freedom.

Oh, yes, you do go on living, but you're living in a jail cell, and pain has the key and refuses to let you out. That's when you pray, "Why are You so far away when I pray? Why do You hide in times of trouble?" (Ps. 10:1, *ELT*).

Pain doesn't treat you humanely as those in American prisons. Pain puts you in a medieval dungeon where you are its victim. Like the medieval jailer, pain will torture you—without pity—down to the last ounce of independence. When you weep and cry, "It's enough," pain will not listen but gives you a few more lashes with the whip. Even when you beg, "Please stop!" pain is the unrelenting torturer who continues to lay the stripes on.

You pray to God, "Why have You forgotten me? Why do I go mourning?" (Ps. 42:9). When you lie sleeplessly in a hospital bed, you know sleep would take away your pain, but it doesn't come. You cry, "How much longer will you forget me, LORD? Forever? . . . How long will sorrow fill my heart day and night?" (Ps. 13:1-2, *GNT*).

You press the call button but the nurse is busy elsewhere; so she doesn't come. You cry out to God for help and He doesn't come. Then you pray, "O my God, I cry in the daytime, but you do not hear; and in the night season, and am not silent" (Ps. 22:2).

When you feel abandoned by God, make sure you're looking for Him in the right place. He's right where He's always been, but you won't find Him inside your complaint.

God calls us to go through situations for a purpose. Out of the hospital God calls us to deal with the death of a loved one, or to deal with financial pressures, or to deal with the things we most fear in life.

Remember, Paul prayed three times to remove a "thorn in the flesh" (see 2 Cor. 12:7-8). Remember, God didn't answer his prayer—just like He doesn't seem to answer your prayers. God was not planning to teach Paul the lesson of deliverance, but rather to teach the important lesson of His grace. Paul had to learn "Not my will but Thine be done," which meant he had to learn to live with his agonizing "thorn." He had to learn the lesson of triumph over suffering. God told him, "My grace is sufficient for thee: for my strength is made perfect in weakness" (2 Cor. 12:9).

In the hospital God has called you to abandon your health, to take what appears to be loneliness. He may be asking you to abandon your physical comfort for physical pain that feels like torture.

Why does God do that? Because God has always demanded death before life. Just as we get eternal life at the death of Jesus Christ, so too we get renewed physical life through the valley of surgery in the shadow of pain.

Doesn't Jesus require death before He brings forth life when He said, "Unless a grain of wheat falls into the ground and dies, it remains alone; but if it dies, it produces much grain" (John 12:24)?

Therefore, you lie in the bed, having abandoned the physical pleasures of life, and through the valley of the shadow of suffering, you move towards renewed physical health. Look again at that verse: "Yea, though I walk through the valley of the shadow of death" (Ps. 23:4). Did you see the word *through*? God not only leads us into the dark night, but also He leads us through darkness and out into the light. So God is with you in your bed of anguish and He can lead you into physical health.

Your doctor, like the Lord, never operates on you to bring pain and hurt to your peaceful existence. No! You go through the operation to find renewed physical life on the other side of your anguish.

So you must pray, "Not my will, but Thine be done." Then remember, abandonment leads to death, and this may mean the death of our pleasures, of our freedom, of our ambitions, or even our immediate happiness.

When you pray, "Not my will but Thine be done," you are not destroying your will; you're not even giving up your will. No! You are surrendering your will to God's will. Your will represents power to make decisions, and if you eradicate your will, then you're nothing but a twig in the current of a stream, being taken where you don't want to go, following the dictates of the current, with no backbone, no determination, no purpose in life.

God does not want to destroy your power of choice; He wants to transform it. God wants you to choose to do His will as you lie in the hospital bed. The will of God for most is to get well. The will of God for some is continual sickness. And the will of God for a few is death.

Therefore, when you pray, "Not my will, but Thine be done," you have voiced the desire of transformation. "Lord, I give my life to You. Now transform me into the image of Jesus Christ—make me like Jesus."

No, God does not destroy our power of choice; He wants to transform it. He wants our will to choose His will—to pursue the plan of God for our life.

Remember that we said in chapter 5 that a positive mental attitude—spiritual therapy—helps the body overcome pain, and eventually helps it to eradicate pain. So when you yield to God's purpose in life, you have taken a step on the path to physical wholeness.

We all know that God is invisible; we can't see Him. So when pain wracks our body, it also influences our thinking. Our prayers of anguish are really prayers of complaint. We don't like what God is doing, and we want Him to come get us out of our suffering. But God is not like a nurse on call who comes running when you press the button. Nor is God like a server in a restaurant who brings coffee to replenish your empty cup. No, He's with us when we can't see Him, and He is working His will when we can't understand it. The problem is always our will as opposed to His will.

In Psalm 77, the writer writhed in anguish, just as you cry out. So your feelings of abandonment are nothing new. Many saints have felt just like you do in your hospital bed and they've prayed the same thing as you've prayed.

Psalm 77

1 I cried out to God with my voice—
To God with my voice;
And He gave ear to me.
2 In the day of my trouble I sought the Lord;
My hand was stretched out in the night without ceasing;
My soul refused to be comforted.
3 I remembered God, and was troubled;
I complained, and my spirit was overwhelmed. Selah

4 You hold my eyelids *open;*
I am so troubled that I cannot speak.
5 I have considered the days of old,
The years of ancient times.
6 I call to remembrance my song in the night;
I meditate within my heart,
And my spirit makes diligent search.

7 Will the Lord cast off forever?
And will He be favorable no more?
8 Has His mercy ceased forever?
Has *His* promise failed forevermore?
9 Has God forgotten to be gracious?
Has He in anger shut up His tender mercies? Selah
(PS. 77:1-7, NKJV)

God didn't take away the writer's suffering because he prayed, nor did God take away the suffering of His people in the wilderness. No, they suffered, but God was with them in their suffering: "God steps through the raging sea and God walks through the overwhelming floods, but God's footprints are not known and are not seen, yet God still leads His people" (Ps. 77:19-20, *ELT*).

So What Should You Do When the Night Comes?

You need to remember to keep doing in the night what you've learned to do in the sunlight: listen and follow God's voice. Isn't that what the writer of the psalm said? "I call to remembrance my song in the night; I meditate within my heart, and my spirit makes diligent search" (Ps. 77:6). Even in dark places, you need a song to put your mind on God and His healing so that you can get your mind off your pain and suffering. You may need music in your room by any type of mechanical device possible: recording, radio, MP3 player, or someone singing.

In May 1999 my mother was dying in the Telfair Hospital, Savannah, Georgia. Her body was swollen with poison and finally her arms became so huge that the nurse could no longer find the vein for the life-giving IV. Finally she was moved to the care of hospice (this is the civilized term that says we've given up all hopes of saving her physically, so we're making her comfortable to die).

There was a Christian nurse who had been converted to Christ in Kingsport Baptist Temple, Kingsport, Tennessee. Now she was living in Savannah, and she had a ministry of singing in churches. But she also sang as she made her rounds in the hospital. Every time she entered my mother's room, she began singing a different Christian song or hymn. Besides the medicine and professional care she gave, her ministry of music always brought a smile to my mother's face, perhaps an inner awareness that God was with her and would walk with her through her personal valley of the shadow of death.

Remember, God never intended for the night to be permanent. He has divided a 24-hour day into light and darkness. So darkness is planned for every person—saved and unsaved—just as God gives the gift of sunlight. So if you're walking in the darkness, you can be assured that morning is coming.

Also, remember that God accomplishes many things in the darkness of night. In the coolness of night, the root systems of plants grow, the dew falls to refresh the leaves, and life breaks forth anew. So, in your darkness, grow those things that are below the surface, things that can't be seen. Just as God has intended to refresh our physical bodies with sleep, so too we must realize that God has a purpose in our night seclusions—so we must learn what those purposes are.

You may feel abandoned and alone; you may even sense deep frustration, but realize, "All things work together for good to those who love God" (Rom. 8:28).

--------- WRAP-UP ---------

Even frustration and forsakenness can be good when they make us yearn for the Lord and search for Him. You may be crying out, "Do not keep silent, O God of my praise!" (Ps. 109:1). Did you see that last part—O God of my praise? You may be like the little boy who cries out, "I'm lost!" And when his father finds him, the dad wipes away his tears. The dad might shed a tear of rejoicing when he finds his lost son, but the dad also remembers the tears of fear that his son might be hurt or that he might not be found. Then comes a warm embrace, and the child experiences the comfort of his father as the father is comforted by his son's presence. So, it's all right to cry out, "I'm lost!" but it's not all right if you refuse the warm embrace of your father who looks after you and wants the best for you.

Note

1. Helen Keller, *The Quotations Page*. http://www.quotationspage.com/subjects/suffer-ing/ (accessed June 2006).

Section Three

WHAT GOD CAN DO FOR HEALING

P ain is a prison that denies life, liberty and the pursuit of happiness. It locks us up into a world of fear and anxiety. It's worse than slavery, for it shackles our hands and binds our feet in stocks. Then pain throws away the key and laughs at our misery.

Chapter 10 tells us we must learn patience when struggling with pain because there is little we can do to speed up the healing process. Chapter 11 gives God's prescription for healing. Sometimes God heals instantaneously, sometimes over a period of time; sometimes it's His will for some to remain sick, or to be an invalid, or to die. Learn the steps to "faith healing" to see if this is for you. Chapter 12 explains the role of faith in moving the mountain-obstacles in your life. Maybe you need more faith to pray for healing. So read to learn how to strengthen your faith.

Chapter 13 explains the role of healing that comes when a loved one, friend or minister visits the sick. Others have a positive role in helping us get well. Chapter 14 is on worship and explains how to make a hospital bed into a sanctuary. When we properly worship God, He will come to bring His presence to our bed of sickness. And isn't His presence what makes a room a sanctuary? Chapter 15 points us to transformation, the ultimate purpose of God when He calls us to suffer.

10

PATIENCE

MENTAL ADJUSTMENT TO LIVING WITH PAIN

*Pain, you just have to ride it out, hope it goes away on its own,
hope the wound that caused it heals. There are no solutions,
no easy answers, you just breathe deep and wait for it to subside.
Most of the time pain can be managed but sometimes the pain gets you
where you least expect it. Hits way below the belt and doesn't let up.
Pain, you just have to fight through, because the truth is you can't
outrun it and life always makes more.*

MEREDITH GREY
(American fictional character, played by actress Ellen Pompeo
on the TV series Grey's Anatomy)[1]

When I left the hospital after my cancer surgery, the orderly put me in a wheelchair and pushed me down to the hospital entrance. With much pain, I got up out of the wheelchair, then had to bend over to get into the front seat of the car. Wow, that hurt! When we finally got home, it was the same distance from my garage to my bedroom as it was from my hospital room to the nurses' station that I had walked each day for the past five days. But when I hurt, it seemed like ten miles.

I faced a long arduous path from pain to full recovery and each step of the path had to be taken patiently. I needed patience.

A pile of get-well cards waited on the nightstand. So, later that afternoon, I began thumbing through them, not paying particular attention to the printed messages. I was more interested in what people penned to me personally.

Then one printed message grabbed my attention, because it annoyed me: "We rejoice in our sufferings" (Rom. 5:3, *RSV*). I spit out the words without thinking, "Hah . . . that's not true!" I thought, *Who in the world is happy because they are suffering?*

The next morning when I began to pray, I remembered the words on that get-well card and read it again. Little did I know that God was trying to teach me something. I looked up the verse in other translations. The *Phillips* translation said, "We can be full of joy here and now even in our trials and troubles."

I knew that God was with me in my sufferings, and I felt He was even holding my hand through my pain. I had even gone so far as to realize that God wanted me to endure my suffering.

But did God want me to rejoice in my suffering? That was asking too much!

I hated my pain and suffered through that first night in the hospital where I measured time in five-minute increments. I kept praying, "Lord, help me make it through the next five minutes."

Pain is not an easy path to walk; it is a path filled with stumbling stones, potholes, and all types of unseen vines to trip us up.

Anyone who has suffered pain knows it's just not pain you have to deal with; it's the fatigue and loss of stamina that you have to endure. You get grumpy and it's easy to gripe about everything. You even complain about people who do kind things for you.

I was blindsided by exhaustion, constantly catnapping during the day. My mind has always been active, and I always want to be doing something. I didn't like being immobile. But even though catnapping interrupted my day, at least it took my mind off my pain.

The worst thing about my pain was that it took away my desire to read, study, or even write. I love to write, whether I am writing books, articles, class notes, or just making notes to myself. And when I hurt too much to write, then I lose the joy of living.

I took a briefcase to the hospital, full of work, but never looked at it once. I brought it home without even opening it. Lying in bed, it was physically overwhelming to just turn my head to look at the clock to see the time.

Time drags when you're recuperating. So when you can't do anything else but heal, what do you need? Patience!

I wanted this painful process to get over with so I could get on with my life. I wanted to start living again without waiting for minutes to tick by.

I prayed, "Lord, will things ever get back the way it used to be? Will I ever write again without my body fighting everything I want to do?"

After two days of being at home, I had Ruth pull me out of bed so I could stand and walk. I walked to my office in the next room and sat at my desk. I spread out a legal pad, opened my Bible, and then picked up a pen to write. But nothing came. Just as a glass is empty, there was nothing in my mind. I couldn't force myself to be creative. I prayed, "Lord, when will I be able to write again?" Then I heard God say, "Patience!"

The longer I sat at my desk, the more intense the pain became. So, I returned to bed. My stomach hurt so badly that I couldn't even lie down by myself. I wrapped my arms around Ruth's neck and she slowly lowered me into bed. When I finally got something for the pain, I slept.

The worst thing about my pain was that it killed my initiative and drive. When I awoke, I prayed again, "Lord, when will I get my initiative back?" God said the same thing again, "Patience!"

That evening, I walked by the open door to my office and the desk looked uninviting. I looked away to think about other things. As I walked toward the kitchen I prayed, "Lord, when will my initiative come back?" Again, God said to me, "Patience!"

Sitting at the kitchen table I finally got the message: God wanted to teach me something about patience. Almost immediately stillness crept into my heart. I didn't think about my pain. I didn't think about anything except that one word: *patience!*

I wanted to pray, "Lord, give me patience and give it *now*," but I knew that wasn't the answer. So I prayed differently, "Lord, I don't know anything about patience." As soon as the words crossed my mind, I found something else happening in my heart: I wanted to learn about patience. Since all of our learning starts with the Bible, I left the kitchen and walked briskly toward my office; and I realized, when you walk with purpose, you don't hurt as much.

I sat at my desk and began looking up the word *patience* in my concordance. The Holy Spirit took control of my mind as I began reading wonderful truths about patience. Paul exhorted the Thessalonians to patience, telling them, "We did not want you to lose heart at the troubles you were going through" (1 Thess. 3:3, *Phillips*). The Holy Spirit showed me that I had lost *heart*, and isn't the heart the place where we love, where we yearn, where we dream of better days? So God was telling me not to lose heart.

Then I read the practical exhortation from James: "Your faith is only put to the test to make you patient, but patience too is to have its practical results so that you will become fully developed, complete, with nothing missing" (Jas. 1:2-4, *Jerusalem Bible*).

That passage made me ashamed of my impatience. Not only was I impatient, but also I had no desire to change. When Ruth and I talked about patience, she always laughed, saying that was the one fruit of the spirit I didn't have.

Then I began to ask myself the question, "Did I have to go through cancer to learn patience?" When I thought about that question, I kept answering myself, "I hope not."

No, I don't think God put me through cancer to only learn patience, although that's one of the things I am beginning to learn. I can't say I've mastered patience yet, but I'm turning the corner. At least I want to be more patient; so I am praying, "Lord, slow me down."

To learn patience I had to pray, "Lord, let happen today what will happen." I had to quit trying to make things happen and let God bring things into my life.

I don't know how I found the verse but I read Jeremiah's words in Lamentations: "He has led me and made [me] walk [in] darkness and not [in] light" (Lam. 3:2). My black hole of suffering was as dark as any time in my life.

Walking in pain is similar to walking in darkness. You don't know where you are going, and you're afraid of smashing your face into a door or bruising your shins on a stool. Walking in darkness is scary, it keeps you on pins and needles, and your heart doesn't have confidence and rest. What's the result of walking in darkness and pain? Anxiety, fear and helplessness.

I read the entire chapter of Lamentations 3. It was then that I rediscovered my life verse: "Great is Thy faithfulness" (Lam. 3:23). Again, I looked at the context where Jeremiah determined, "Great is Thy faithfulness." Jeremiah reminded me, "It is of the Lord's mercies that we are not consumed"—meaning that God is merciful not to eat us up with pain or to destroy us. So, I began to thank God for answering prayers about my operation experience.

Before going into surgery, I was told that the doctor would probably cut out a section of my colon. When he talked about sewing the colon back together, I had asked, "What happens if the two edges don't perfectly heal and grow back together?" The doctor told me about the dangers of leakage into the body cavity, so I prayed for the doctor to sew perfectly the colon back together. After completion of the surgery, there was no indication of leakage, so I thanked God for answers to prayer. Before I went into the hospital, I realized that there are many more germs in the hospital than any other place. So I asked God to keep me from any germs, bacteria or any influence that would make me sicker or to cause any other life-threatening conditions. God answered, so I began to thank God for His faithfulness.

I went through a whole list of things that I had prayed, and I realized God brought me successfully through the operation. Even though I had pain, I could paraphrase the words of Jeremiah: "It is of the Lord's mercies that we are not destroyed through operation mistakes." Why did God see me successfully through the operation? "Because His compassions fail not, they are new every morning" (Lam. 3:22-23). God loves me every day; and as I was getting stronger each day, I found God using His promises through Jeremiah to make me more patient.

In my bed of suffering, I began to sing softly, "Great is Thy faithfulness." And singing helped me bear my pain and make it through my suffering.

What is patience teaching me? It's teaching me I was wrong to demand from God reasons why I got cancer. I was wrong to demand of God reasons why I hurt. I was wrong to demand of God reasons for anything.

So I was learning patience, but what about that *joy* thing? As I read through my concordance, I found that Paul said, "Patience with joy" (Col. 1:11).

The problem was that much of my patience was like gritting my teeth or sitting motionless as I drummed my fingers on the table. I thought that was patience. But it was only human patience; it was not patience with joy. So I looked up the passage in the *Living Bible* and found that it said, "So that you can keep on going no matter what happens, always full of the joy of the Lord" (Col. 1:11). The key to patience is to get joy from the Lord.

I remembered the words of my wife when she had said, "Elmer, patience is not one of your strong gifts." And she'd always said, "When God passed out the fruit of the Spirit, you didn't get patience."

Notice what Paul actually said about this fruit: "But when the Holy Spirit controls our lives, he will produce this kind of fruit in us: love, joy, peace, patience" (Gal. 5:22, *NLT*). Did you see that last fruit—patience?

The fruit of the Spirit, like fruit on this earth, must grow normally, gradually and quietly. Growing takes time! Therefore, it's going to take time for me to grow the fruit of patience. So my suffering was helping me to grow patience and now I was willing to grow it with joy (see Col. 1:11).

So, where does that leave me? It means I can't grow my patience; God must do it. Notice that patience is a fruit of the Spirit. It's the Holy Spirit's job to grow the fruit of patience in my life. And what soil was He using to grow this fruit? He was using the soil of suffering that came from cancer surgery. So I had to willingly accept my pain—with joy—so that the Holy Spirit could grow His fruit of patience in my life.

I used to grow tomatoes on the back deck of my house. After I planted tomatoes, watered them and put fertilizer on them, what could I do to make them grow? Nothing! I guess I had to patiently wait for them to grow. Now the Holy Spirit had brought adversity into my life and what could I do about it? Nothing! I had to yield to the Holy Spirit to let Him build patience in my life. In the great wisdom of the Holy Spirit, He chose to teach me patience—with joy—through suffering.

When you're trapped in the black hole of pain, there is nothing you can do about being trapped. It's like being in jail. But even in jail you have a choice: you can choose to accept your confinement willingly and learn from it, or you can choose to fight your imprisonment and grow bitter.

——————— WRAP-UP ———————

I had no idea that God would use my suffering to help me grow as a Christian. So my pain was good because it caused me to become a patient Christian so that others could see Christ in me.

I had always thought that we grow in Christ by reading the Word, praying, witnessing and being a good testimony. Never had I thought that God could use pain to grow patience in my life as the fruit of the Spirit. And to compound that difficulty, never did I think God would use my suffering to grow patience with joy.

Note

1. Meredith Grey, *ThinkExist.com*. http://en.thinkexist.com/quotations/pain/15.html (accessed June 2006).

11

PRAYER

GOD'S PRESCRIPTION FOR
HEALING PRAYER

When pain of the world surrounds us with darkness and despair,
When searching just confounds us with false hopes ev'rywhere,
When lives are starved for meaning and destiny is bare,
We are called to follow Jesus and let God's healing flow through us.

JIM STRATHDEE,
TWENTIETH-CENTURY HYMN-WRITER[1]

I believe that God heals in answer to the "prayer of faith" (Jas. 5:15). On April 24, 1985, I was getting ready for chapel at Liberty University when someone announced to the university leaders that our dean of students, Vernon Brewer, had cancer and was only given six weeks to six months to live.

When Jerry Falwell entered the room, he was told about Vernon's condition. Because Vernon was such an outstanding dean of students, Falwell said, "We can't let Vernon die! We've got to pray for a miracle." He looked around the room at all of us and said, "We've got to pray to change God's mind."[2]

That statement sounds preposterous when examined at face value. However, remember that there were many times when God's people prayed against the reluctance of God. Sometimes God tests His people by not answering prayer, or by waiting to see if people demonstrate their faith by continual fasting and prayer. I believe that was God's challenge to the entire Liberty University family.

Falwell didn't have a well-planned strategy; he immediately walked to the chapel platform and began publicly making plans (I call this the leading of the Holy Spirit). Falwell announced, "Tomorrow I want all 5,000 students to fast—go only without eating—and pray for the healing of Vernon Brewer." He explained that each person could drink liquids but could not eat any solid food. He suggested a Yom Kippur fast, which means not eating the evening meal, nor breakfast or lunch. That's a one-day fast using God's prescription in Genesis 1: "the evening and the morning were the first day" (Gen. 1:5).

Then Falwell said that he wanted every student to pray at least one hour nonstop for Vernon's healing. He quoted the words of Jesus in Matthew 26:40: "Could you not watch with Me one hour?" Falwell noted that he didn't want students just praying at the beginning of class or as they walked about campus, but rather he wanted them to go to the Worley Prayer Chapel and spend an hour there, praying for the healing of Vernon Brewer.

Next Falwell announced, "I want a large prayer calendar printed as quickly as possible and placed on this large wall," and he pointed to the gigantic doors in the Schilling Center. He asked every student to sign up for an hour on the 24-hour prayer clock so they would commit themselves to praying.

As Falwell was making plans publicly, he asked that the school cafeteria be shut down. A few minutes later someone whispered in his ear that there were diabetics who needed to eat, and perhaps there were some students who wouldn't fast; therefore, they should not be forced to go without food. So Falwell said, "If any of you has a health reason why you have to eat, there will be a skeleton crew in the kitchen to provide a meal for you. (Only 50 students out of 5,000 showed up to eat in the cafeteria.)

Then Falwell called on the school officials to come to the platform to offer public prayer for Vernon's healing. I was standing next to Vernon on the platform and God said to me, "Place your hands on Vernon's head and pray for his healing." I didn't hear an audible voice, but there was a deep impression in my heart to pray for Vernon. My first reaction was to say, "No, people will think I am a Pentecostal if I do it."

Almost immediately I was stunned by my unbelief. I recalled a statement I had said in a sermon: "You can't call Him Lord and say no to Him."

Instantly, I asked God to forgive me and placed my hands on Vernon's head and began praying for his healing. A deep feeling of assurance came over my heart that God would heal Vernon Brewer. I didn't feel a tingle in my hand, nor any heat; it was just an inner assurance of the Holy Spirit witnessing to my Spirit of what God intended to do. I believe that inner conviction describes the prayer of faith—when you know you'll get an answer before it happens.

I do not claim credit for praying for Vernon's healing. I believe the credit goes to 5,000 students who prayed. From that experience I learned the valuable lesson that there is value in the volume of prayer.

When more than two people agree together, then fast and pray together, God will hear and answer (see Matt. 18:19).

Praying for Healing

Look at God's exhortation through James: "Is anyone among you suffering? Let him pray . . . Is any among you sick? Let him call for the elders of the church, and let them pray over him, anointing him with oil in the name of the Lord" (Jas. 5:13-14).

Notice that the first thing James says to do when we are suffering is to pray. He asks the questions "Is any suffering?" and "Is any sick?" In answer to these questions, he directs prayer about our suffering and pain.

Second, since you are sick you should call for the elders of the church to pray over you. This involves your pastor, or visitation pastor, or the members or the church board. Notice that you are to call them, not the reverse. Therefore, I am leery of the faith healer who comes to town and calls for sick people to come to his meeting. The opposite is commanded: "Call for the elders" (Jas. 5:14). The Bible specifies "elders," meaning more than one should pray over you. There is value in the volume of prayer (see Matt. 18:19); therefore, call a plurality of elders.

Why does God want you to call elders of the church? Because they are your shepherds and they generally know whether you have been faithful to God or not. Perhaps they may know some sin in your life, or places where you've been unfaithful. They know your faithfulness in church attendance and tithing. Elders should not pray over you until they first deal with any sin in your life that might be your cause of suffering.

There is a third thing the sick person should do: "Confess [your] trespasses to one another, and pray for one another, that you may be healed" (Jas. 5:16). And what does this verse mean? That we must first confess our sins before we pray for healing. So you've been in the hospital bed begging God to relieve your pain. Have you dealt with your sin? Is there a sin in your past that is blocking your fellowship with God? You may need to deal with sin because it might keep you from being healed.

If you have a sin, you must confess it ultimately to God. You don't confess it to the one praying with you, but to God because He's the One to forgive you. Remember what was promised: "If we confess our sins, He is faithful and just to forgive us [our] sins and to cleanse us from all unrighteousness" (1 John 1:9).

Obviously, you confess your sins to God. But why does the text say, "confess your sins, one to another"? Probably this means that the elders should counsel you back into fellowship with God. It doesn't mean that elders can forgive trespasses; it only means that when you are honest with your church leadership, it's indicative that you are honest with God. Then you're in the position to pray for healing.

Notice the fourth step for healing: The elders are to "pray over him." I think it is important when pastors pray for healing that they lay hands on the head or shoulder of the person for whom they are praying. Obviously, I don't believe there is a transfer of power by touching, nor do I believe anything magical happens in the touch. The touch is an outward obedience to an inner desire. You want to identify with the person, so you lay hands on him as an act of identification that the two of you are agreeing together for healing. "If two of you agree on earth concerning anything that they ask, it will be done for them by My Father in heaven" (Matt. 18:19).

The next step is to anoint the sick person with oil. At my church, Pastor Charlie Harbin keeps olive oil in his office desk. He does not take it with him to the hospital; he waits for the person in the hospital to ask for the anointing of oil. Therefore, in my church we would not take the initiative to anoint sick people. The sick person must first have faith that God can heal, then take the initiative to request anointing.

Some churches keep anointing oil in the pulpit so that when people come to the church altar to pray for healing, the oil is available. That is a wonderful act of faith on the part of the church. Some pastors carry their oil in their pocket when they visit in the hospital, because a patient may ask to be anointed. That also is a wonderful act of faith.

What kind of oil should be used? John Calvin taught in his commentary that one of the elders of the church would probably be a physician; therefore, they were anointed with medicinal oil to clean out the wound and bring about therapy. I don't think this is what this text means. Some spiritualize the text to say that oil is simply the presence of the Holy Spirit that flows in to heal. I don't think that is what the text means. I believe that oil means oil, and that's all that oil means.

I don't think God is concerned about the type of oil that you use. I've already said that we use olive oil at my church. I know that on occasions when oil was not available a pastor used cooking oil to make the anointing. I even heard the ridiculous suggestion that one pastor used "3-in-1 oil." What am I trying to say? God is not interested in the type of oil we use; God is interested in our inward obedience to His Word and our expression of faith in Him that He can heal. And isn't that the bottom line? Do you really believe God can heal you?

There are two or three other points that ought to be made about the prayer of healing. First, sometimes you don't pray for healing; you pray for God to guide and diagnose correctly what is the cause of your pain. Then you pray for the doctor to correctly prescribe the medication that will take away the pain. Next, you pray for the body to heal itself; and finally, you pray for divine interruption in the disease so that God takes away the cause of sickness.

My primary prayer partner is Buddy Bryant, who lives in Nelson County, Virginia, and owns a six-man timber-cutting business. He cuts timber for the paper mill.

Buddy gets up at 4:00 AM every morning and prays until 5:00 and I am his primary target of intercession. Then he says that when he is standing over a fallen tree, stripping away the branches with a power saw, since he can't talk to anyone over the buzz of the saw, he uses that time to pray for me.

Recently, Buddy's wife, Alice, went to the doctor with medical problems. The doctor diagnosed her with Lupus and began a prescribed medicine to deal with the disease and pain.

I meet with approximately 12 to 18 prayer partners early every Sunday morning to intercede for my ministry to the Pastor's Bible Class at Thomas Road Baptist Church, and other aspects of our church. Buddy meets with me in that prayer group. We prayed diligently for Alice's healing. Rather than getting better, she got worse. We couldn't understand what God was doing.

Finally, Alice went to a university medical center in Richmond, Virginia, to see a specialist, who said, "I don't see any trace of Lupus!" The unbelievers immediately assumed that the first doctor made a wrong diagnosis. But those in my prayer circle said, "No, God healed her of Lupus, and the medicine she was given for Lupus was causing her sickness. She no longer needed the medicine that was making her sick."

However, the second doctor did find a type of creeping arthritis, and now we've made that a matter of prayer. So what does this story tell us? We must pray specifically for the doctor's correct diagnosis and correct prescription of medicine.

When you meet the above conditions, then you are able to enter into the prayer of faith, which is believing God for an answer before it comes. At this moment faith kicks in and God intervenes. Remember, "Without faith it is impossible to please

Him" (Heb. 11:6). So when you please God—you worship God—with your confidence, He then responds.

Guidelines for Praying for the Sick

1. Learn to ask questions before you pray for healing.
Sometimes we are quick to pray, but we pray for the wrong thing, at the wrong time, or even for the wrong results. The Bible calls this "We ask amiss" (Jas. 4:3).

Years ago I was phoning an absentee in my Sunday school class when the lady told me she was staying home from church to take care of her invalid mother. Then she added, "She is very sick." I impetuously responded, "Let me pray for her that God would heal her and raise her up." The woman answered, "Oh, no!" She explained that her mother had lost the use of many of her physical organs and could no longer communicate; the family was praying for an easy death.

If I had asked questions first or if I had listened, I would have known how to pray intelligently. When I learned the problem, I prayed for "dying grace." This is when God gives us grace to accept our death, we pass from this earth in spiritual rest, and our death glorifies God.

John Wesley said of the early Methodists, "We Methodists die well." By that he meant that Methodists held on to their faith to the end, but they died with dignity, giving praise to God. Oh, that we all would learn that lesson.

2. Practice listening to hurting people before you begin praying for them.
When Jesus entered the area of the Bethesda Pool, tradition tells us that there were between 2,000 and 3,000 people waiting for the stirring of the water so that they could enter the pool. They believed, "Whoever stepped in first, after the stirring of the water, was made well of whatever disease he had" (John 5:4).

Notice that when Jesus entered the arena of those suffering people, He didn't try to get their attention or motivate them for healing. No, Jesus walked straight to one—only one—and asked, "Do you want to be made well?" (John 5:6). This question sounds condescending because everyone at the Pool of Bethesda wanted to be healed. Obviously that's why the man was there.

But Jesus was not asking for information. He was asking to stir up a desire in the man to be healed. He was asking to stir up the man's faith.

Notice the man's response: "Sir, I have no man to put me into the pool when the water is stirred up; but while I am coming, another steps down before me" (John 5:7). Isn't that just like all of us? We always make excuses.

Let's examine the lame man's excuses.

The Lame Man's Excuses	Our Excuses
"I have no man."	Using people as an excuse rather than depending upon God.
"When the water is stirred."	Using conditions as an excuse. This is dependence upon circumstances rather than on God.
"To put me in the pool."	Geographic excuses. This is an excuse of place— why we do not obey God.
"While I am coming, another steps down before me."	The excuse of partiality. God rewards first come, first served.
"Now it was the Sabbath."	This is the excuse of time. People thought God only does miracles at certain times.

3. *Strengthen your faith so you can pray in faith.*
When the Bible exhorts the sick to "pray for one another" (Jas. 5:16), it is saying that you should make a commitment to pray for others as well as for your pain. The word for prayer is *euché*, which is a "vow of prayer." Basically, this means that we should make a commitment or promise to pray for other people, as we ask them to pray for us.

And as we see God working in other lives in response to our prayer, we are strengthened to believe God can heal our own painful conditions.

4. *Don't be vague when you pray.*
Doesn't the Bible teach us, "You do not have because you do not ask" (Jas. 4:2)? Maybe the doctor doesn't make the right diagnosis because you haven't asked the Spirit of God to show him something that is beyond his limited observation. Maybe the doctor prescribes the wrong medication because you haven't prayed for God to guide the doctor in writing the prescription. The same thing in surgery: you should pray for God to guide the incision of the scalpel as well as the final suturing up of the wound.

When I faced surgery, I had heard that there are more germs in the hospital than in any other place on earth. I also heard that you can get infection easier in the hospital than any other place on earth. I don't know if these two statements are true (hospitals do more to protect their patients from germs than any other institution). However, I prayed specifically before my surgery that God would keep me from any type of infection, both in surgery and in rehabilitation. I asked specifically, "God, raise up a hedge of protection against germs of infection so that I might come out of this surgery healthy."

———— WRAP-UP ————

James ends his discussion of faith healing with an example from the life of Elijah: "The effective, fervent prayer of a righteous man avails much. Elijah was a man with a nature like ours, and he prayed earnestly that it would not rain; and it did not rain on the land for three years and six months. And he prayed again, and the heaven gave rain, and the earth produced its fruit" (Jas. 5:16-18). The phrase "effective, fervent" comes from the Greek work *energo*, which is "energized." This means that when you've met the above conditions, then you have lots of energy or emotions to pray for healing.

Don't miss the phrase "avails much"; it's from the Greek *ischuo*, which means "strong." It could mean that when you meet the conditions of prayer, the intercessor becomes a "strong" prayer warrior. But it could also refer to the sick person getting stronger.

So examine the conditions for healing. First, it has to be the prayer of a "righteous man." Maybe you haven't gotten healing because a "righteous" man didn't pray for you. Maybe you're not righteous, nor is the one who is praying for you.

Second, to get healing, there had to be "fervent prayer," which means to pour out your soul to God (see Ps. 62:8). You must pray sincerely, constantly, wholeheartedly and diligently. Are those characteristics the way you pray for healing? So, believe in fervent prayer, believe in the prescription for healing, and believe in God. He can do it.

Notes

1. Jim Strathdee, "We are Called to Follow Jesus," *Everflowing Streams* (1981), 1. 1-4, Desert Flower Music, Ridgecrest, CA (1978). http://www.poemhunter.com/quotations/destiny/page-12/ (accessed April 2006).

2. This is called "praying against the reluctance of God." God told Moses he would not go with Israel to the Promised Land because of Israel's sin. Moses interceded, even praying, "Yet now, if You will forgive their sin—but if not, I pray, blot me out of Your book which You have written" (Exod. 32:32). Then God relented, "My Presence will go [with you,]" (Exod. 33:14).

12

FAITH

TO MOVE A MOUNTAIN
OF PAIN

*Seeds of faith are always within us; sometimes it takes a crisis
to nourish and encourage their growth.*

SUSAN TAYLOR[1]

Pain is like a flat tire on a deserted road in the middle of the night. You no longer can go where you used to go, and you no longer can do the things you used to do. As a matter of fact, when a tire blows in the middle of the night, you usually panic and think, *What am I going to do?* or *Who can help me?*

So you're stuck in bed and you're not going anywhere soon. "You've got a flat tire!" What are you going to do? When you can't do anything else, you can call on God.

The first thing to remember is that *prayer is a relationship.* The most used word in the Greek language for prayer is *proseuchomai.* It comes from two Greek words: (1) the preposition *pros,* which means *towards,* and (2) *euchomai,* which means *face.* Therefore, prayer is looking into the face of God—establishing a personal relationship with Him. You can do this when you're stuck in bed.

Second, *realize that prayer is about God and His purpose for your life.* People think that prayer begins and ends with asking. So they begin praying, "Lord, help me. Take away this pain." Notice that this person didn't begin by confessing their sins to establish a relationship with God. Nor did they worship God to feel His presence with them in their pain. They treat prayer like sanctified begging, "Please help me . . ."

Prayer is not primarily to get you through your pain, or to even answer any request you may have about your suffering. When you bow your head, remember, it's all about relationship!

When you begin to pray, search for the purpose God wants you to learn while you're in pain, trying to understand His will for your life. "Therefore do not be unwise, but understand what the will of the Lord is" (Eph. 5:17). Since God tells us to know His will, then believe that He will show you His will. Therefore, the first step of prayer is not about getting rid of pain. Just because God wants to show you His will, that does not mean you will understand it immediately. Ask God to show you His will and show you what to do.

The third thing you must do in your prayers is to yield to God's will. You must pray, "Thy will be done" (Matt. 6:10, *KJV*).

David prayed, "lead me, O Lord" (Ps. 5:8), and to make sure, he asked God to help him understand the path: "Lead me in a plain path" (Ps. 27:10). Sometimes God won't show you His will for the entire trip you must take. God's will is sometimes like the headlights on your car where you can only see approximately 50 yards into the darkness. God only shows you His will for the next couple of days—and it involves more pain. But each time you go another 50 yards, God shows you the next 50 yards; then He may show you next week when the pain goes away and you leave the hospital. God leads some people day by day. God shows other people what it will be like when they go back to work.

In the hospital the doctor told me to get up and walk to the nurses' station some 30 feet away. To me, that was an impossibility; I could barely walk to the bathroom, which was less than 10 steps. But within a couple of days, I was able to walk to the nurses' station, and a couple more days later I could do it 3 times a day. Six months later I walked 18 holes of golf. But that first day when I hurt so badly, I wondered if I would ever walk again without pain.

So what does that mean for your prayer life? God may not show you His entire will; you may have to search for it. We should apply Jesus' invitation to prayer like this: "Pray—keep on praying; seek—keeping on seeking; knock—keep on knocking" (Matt. 7:7, *ELT*).

In another place Paul tells us, "Pray without ceasing" (1 Thess. 5:17, *KJV*). Again the original language gives us great insight in how to pray: "Pray continually in an intermittent way" (1 Thess. 5:17, *ELT*). The original language suggests that "praying without ceasing" means to pray intermittently like the windshield wipers on my car that operate only when water splashes on the windshield. When they are not needed, the windshield wiper goes off. But when they're needed, they turn on automatically without my touching the switch. What does that mean to prayer? Every time you have a need, pray intermittently. Sometimes you'll have to ask God to make it through an intense moment of pain. At other times your pain is not constant, so you ignore it.

Spending a lot of time in prayer builds up your faith to trust God for bigger things. Jesus said, "Whatever things you ask in prayer, believe and you will receive" (Matt. 21:22). Sometimes the more you pray, the stronger your faith becomes. And when your faith becomes mature, God answers miraculously. Yes, there have been times when people have been healed because there was "the prayer of faith" (Jas. 5:15). And what happens when you pray the prayer of faith? God may "raise up the sick" (Jas. 5:15).

Next, obey Jesus by bringing your prayer requests to Him. Jesus promised, "Whatever you ask in My name, that I will do" (John 14:13). So when you don't pray about your sickness, you are not obedient. What does that mean? "You do not have because you do not ask" (Jas. 4:2). God may not answer your prayer for healing because you don't meet all His conditions. And what are the conditions to answered prayer?

- We must ask sincerely.
- We must ask continually.
- We must ask according to Scripture.
- We must ask in Jesus' name.

- We must ask in faith, knowing we will receive.
- We must ask according to the will of God.
- We must ask after repenting of our sins.

Notice that it probably takes most of the above seven conditions to get prayers answered about healing. It may not be the will of God to heal you, so you must pray, "Thy will be done." It may be the will of God to give you stamina and patience to deal with your pain. It may be the will of God to give wisdom to your doctor to counteract your infection. It may be the will of God to put a "hedge about you" so that disease and germs cannot get to you (Job 1:10).

Sometimes we must deal with the issue of unbelief when praying for healing. Jesus said, "Whatever things you ask when you pray, believe that you receive them, and you will have them" (Mark 11:24). So faith is one condition to get healing from your sickness. However, look at all the conditions to make sure you are praying in harmony with the will of God.

What happens when you don't have enough faith? Then you should pray what the disciples requested when they needed faith: "Increase our faith" (Luke 17:5). The father told Jesus that the disciples could not heal his son. Jesus later said to the disciples that they couldn't heal because it was their lack of faith. So you need to pray as the father prayed: "Lord, I believe; help my unbelief!" (Mark 9:24). This means you can overcome unbelief. You can ask for more faith so you can pray for bigger things.

Remember, God answers all pray but He answers them in three different ways:

- God gives you your request.
- God says, "No."
- God says, "Wait."

Sometimes I add a fourth answer for God when He hears the ridiculous things we ask: "You've got to be kidding!"

The key to getting answers to prayer is to ask for things that God has promised to give. He promised to give wisdom (see Jas.

1:2-4), so you can ask for wisdom for the doctor to prescribe medicine and operate. You can ask for wisdom to do His will in your life. I've found that throughout my life, the closer my request gets to the Bible, the more likely God hears my request and gives me answers.

WRAP-UP

Don't forget that sin in your life will block your ability to pray: "We know that God does not hear sinners" (John 9:31). Also, when I plan to sin, God won't hear me: "If I regard iniquity in my heart, the Lord will not hear" (Ps. 66:18). Also, when you ask for things that are selfish, God is not going to hear you: "And even when you do ask, you don't get it because your whole motive is wrong—you want only what will give you pleasure" (Jas. 4:3, *NLT*). Therefore, if you want to accomplish everything that God has for you, then you must give attention to your prayer life. Remember that Jesus said, "You must always pray" (Luke 18:1).

Note

1. Susan Taylor, *The Quotations Page*. http://www.quotationspage.com/search.php3? homesearch=faith&page=8 (accessed June 2006).

13

PRESENCE

NOTHING HELPS HURTING LIKE
TALKING TO A FRIEND

Pain is real when you get other people to believe in it.
If no one believes in it but you, your pain is madness or hysteria.

NAOMI WOLF[1]

People who are in the deepest pain often feel as though God has deserted them. They feel alone, frustrated and fearful, "Where are You, God?"

The greatest thing you can do for someone in pain is to spend time with him—give him your presence. More than buying expensive flowers, or bringing him a book to read, or some other expensive gift, you can help someone in pain by just being there.

When people cry out, "Where is God when I'm in pain?" do they really know what they are asking? What do they honestly expect? Do they expect Jesus to show up at the foot of the bed? Or do they expect Him to come sit beside them and listen to their pain? People cry out for God's presence, but they're not sure what He will do when He gets there.

When we're in pain, God does come to visit us, but He comes in ways we don't expect. He comes in the flesh of those who come to be with us. God sends His representation—people—who come alongside to be there for us. This could be a pastor, friend, family member or a fellow worker from our job. Grandparents are wonderful representatives from God.

When someone is hurting, do they want counseling or encouragement? No! What they want is for the pain to go away. But it doesn't go away, so what do they want from God or from His agents? Comfort!

Technically, there is nothing most of us can do for the hurting because we're not doctors. We've not been trained in diagnoses, therapy or healing. So there is very little you can say to help them. But your presence may mean more to them when they hurt and can't get relief.

Remember the story of Job, who lost his children, wealth and servants? Next, he lost his health. Then three friends came to "cheer him up." Notice what they did when they first arrived. They sat silently for seven days before they said anything. Technically, these three friends started right (even though they ended up wrong) because they didn't begin by questioning or attacking Job. They just sat there for seven days. If you're hurting, that's the best thing a friend can give you: time, sympathy and a listening ear. They can give you themselves.

God uses His representatives who come alongside to say, "We're here for you. You're not alone. We will bear the pain with you."

When someone comes to visit, it makes little difference what they say; rather, the most important things are availability and presence. Just being with them tells the person in pain that they are not alone.

So if you have a friend in pain, don't change. Don't put on a ministerial tone and say, "God understands." What you need to do is just understand.

If your friendship is about sports, talk about sports. If your friendship is about work, or the church, or a hobby, talk about that. Be the kind of friend in pain that you were to them before pain knocked on the door.

Think about it. When someone is in the valley of the shadow of death, everything changes. They no longer have confidence, they're filled with fear, and they can't do what they used to do. And surely the hospital room is not their room at home. They need to know that your friendship has not changed in their world that has been knocked topsy-turvy.

What else can you give them besides your presence? You can pray for them when you're together and apart. If you believe in prayer, then prayer is a great gift to give to them.

Another gift is hope. When a person is alone and hurting, they are eaten up with anxiety and they may be scared of the future. So what can you give them? You can give them hope for every tomorrow they'll face. So talk about what the two of you will do together when they're well. Talk about what the sick person is going to accomplish when they get out of the hospital. Talk about life that will go on, and that they will be a part of that life that will go on. Give them hope.

You can also give them "silent understanding." Sometimes words are not the best tools in a hospital room. Only the callous person will say, "I know what you're going through—I had that operation once." No! No one in the world knows what is in the heart of the person who is going through excruciating pain. You don't know what they feel like. You don't know their fears. You don't know any unconfessed sin with which they are dealing.

When I laid in a hospital room with a 15-inch incision down my abdomen, I hurt like never before in my life. I stared at the clock and divided my dark night into five-minute segments. I just tried to get through every five minutes. I constantly pushed back the pain and tried to think about something else. But it didn't work. Pain was an aggressive intruder that kept demanding my attention.

Jerry Falwell came to see me. He talked about how we first began Liberty University, but I don't remember what he said. He prayed for me and I forget his exact words, but right as he left the room he said, "Elmer, a week from now all your sufferings will be a bad dream."

"Yes," I said in my heart. About 20 years ago I had the pain of three broken ribs and it had gone away. So I realized that the pain from my cancer surgery would also go away. At the time I couldn't even turn over in bed, but my heart leaped out of the bed to grab hold of those words of hope and to hang on for dear life. Those words from my pastor were my hope of life after pain.

And you know what? My pastor was right. A week later my surgery was a bad dream.

How Your Presence Can Help

- Let medical personnel treat physical pain and other symptoms so that pastors and families can focus on relationships and spiritual renewal.

- Be emotionally and spiritually "present" in the face of suffering and despair.

- Help the patient identify spiritual, relational and emotional goals or tasks that give them hope.

- Notice opportunities for healing and spiritual renewal that the patient and family might overlook.

- Share stories of how other patients and families have found meaning, hope and healing during this time of life.

WRAP-UP

So if you're in pain and your friends visit, what can you expect from them? You appreciate the flowers, and you read the get-well cards, and you even eat some of the candy; and then what? What can you get that is more beneficial than anything else? Friendship. They can be the kind of friend in your pain that you were to them before you began to suffer. They can be themselves.

Note

1. Naomi Wolfe (b. 1962), U.S. author, "Violence," *The Beauty Myth*, 1990. http://www.bartleby.com/66/99/65199.html (accessed March 2006).

14

WORSHIP

THE POSITIVE DIVERSION OF PAIN

The deepest level of worship is praising God in spite of pain,
thanking God during a trial, trusting him when tempted, surrendering
when suffering, and loving him when he seems distant.

RICK WARREN[1]

The most outstanding thing about Job was his patience: "Be-hold, we count them happy which endure. Ye have heard of the patience of Job" (Jas. 5:11, *KJV*). He was incredibly rich, called the "richest person in that entire area" (Job 1:3, *NLT*). At the beginning of the book of Job, it lists all of his wealth by houses, cattle, lands, servants, and a wonderful family.

Job seems to epitomize the worldly thinking of that day and today: "Those who obey and remain faithful to God will be re-warded by God." In contrast, don't many Christians believe that "Those who sin and rebel against God are punished by God"?

But here's an enigma surrounded by a paradox: Job was righteous but suffered, and he speaks of those who are evil yet prosper. How can that be?

Of all of the men in the land of Nod (the northern part of the Sinai Peninsula), Job was the most upright in his business dealings and the most godly in his walk with the Lord. If ever you were to point out a good role model, you could say, "Do you see Job? Go and live like him."

But a debate took place in heaven, and Job was not asked to take part in that discussion. Job didn't even know it was going on. Satan accused God that Job loved Him only because "You have put a hedge around him" and "You have made him rich." Satan was telling God that Job obeyed Him only because God had made him wealthy, happy and there were no problems in his life. Satan's accusation was an attack on the impeccable character of God. The Devil was suggesting that Job only loved God because of the money and things he got from God.

We hear that criticism sometimes today about our churches. The critics say we just bribe children to come to Sunday school by giving them an award or a prize. It's the same thing that Satan said about Job: "God bribed him for his love and service."

The book of Job demonstrates how a servant can be faithful to God in the face of suffering, criticism and betrayal. Didn't Job's wife betray him when she said, "Curse God and die!" (Job 2:9)?

Up until Job lost everything, he seemed to have always believed in a just and fair God. But he was perplexed when he lost everything. The minus and plus columns just didn't add up. Something was wrong.

As a result Job cried out like I cry out: "Why me? Why this? Why now?" Those are the universal questions when anyone suffers. They want to know why.

You remember that Job's three friends came to visit him. I believe that one was Job's uncle, another was his great-uncle, and the third was his great-great-uncle once removed. And like cantankerous old uncles, they accused Job of hiding something from them. So Job had to debate with his uncles the plight of his suffering, and in that debate we see Job analyzing his suffering.

As you read the arguments in the book of Job, and trace what the men say to one another, you explore the mysterious reason of pain. Why God allowed pain is never revealed in the book of Job. God has hidden the enigma of suffering from our sight.

What did the uncles say to Job? First, they said that no one suffers without a reason, so the three uncles reasoned that God was just. He treated everyone fairly if they obeyed and remained faithful to Him. So the uncles began to probe with their questions: "Job, have you sinned? Surely your suffering means that you have sinned." Therefore they came to the conclusion that

"God punishes those who sin; therefore God is punishing Job because of hidden sin."

Job's Problems

- Inflamed ulcerous sores (Job 2:7)
- Persistent itching (Job 2:8)
- Facial disfiguration (Job 2:12)
- Loss of appetite (Job 3:24)
- Fears and depression (Job 3:25)
- Sores that burst open, scabbed over, cracked and oozed with pus (Job 7:5)
- Worms grew in the sores themselves (Job 7:5)
- Difficulty in breathing (Job 9:18)
- A darkening of the eyelid (Job 16:16)
- Loss of weight (Job 19:20)
- Continual pain (Job 30:27)
- High fever with chills and diarrhea[2]

So what do the uncles want Job to do? They want him to confess his sin so that God can forgive Job and relieve Job of his pain and misery. But Job declares that there is no hidden sin in his life. The uncles make an accusation against his character: "You're lying." Job knows differently; he knows his heart. He knows that he has lived righteously, and that he can't deny God by any stretch of the imagination.

As you read the answers of Job, you see that at times he waivers in his confidence and questions God. Probably the same why question is uttered in almost every hospital room by godly saints. So Job is no different. Sometimes Job argues with his uncles and at other times accuses them of lying, just as they accused him of not telling the truth.

Job points out that men who steal prosper and grow fat. Then he examines the opposite—that godly men live in poverty, and many of them suffer pain like himself. So what is Job's conclusion? Both good and evil men prosper, and both good and evil men suffer pain.

Even in his pain, Job continues to justify himself, thinking he does not deserve his tragedy. But even when he questions why he is suffering, Job never abandons his loyalty to God. He cries out, "Though he slay me, yet will I trust him" (Job 13:15).

Suffering and Free Will

Before we quickly criticize Job's friends for their conclusions, there is an abundance of references in the Bible to indicate that God does punish sin. Doesn't the Bible teach, "For whatever a man sows, that he will also reap" (Gal. 6:7)? Also, don't Christians quote the Scripture, "The wages of sin is death" (Rom. 3:23)? Many times the prophets preached that if Israel didn't repent, God would judge them by a plague of locusts, or they would be plundered by a foreign army, or they would suffer disastrous results from natural calamities. Isn't that a case of God punishing sin? So what is different about the three uncles? They were simply saying what was taught in the preponderance of scriptural evidence: "For whatever a man sows, that he will also reap. For he who sows to his flesh will of the flesh reap corruption" (Gal. 6:7-8).

If there's any vindication here, it's that we can't always apply a general principle to a specific action. Job suffered, but not because he was unrighteous. Why can't we just realize that suffering is a fact as sure as germs cause disease? If you eat green oranges, you'll get a stomachache. If you roll off the roof of a house, you'll fall downward. Most of our suffering has nothing to do with our righteousness or unrighteousness. We suffer sickness because we're exposed to germs. We suffer cancer because of cancer cells in our body. We cry over broken ribs because of an accident. We are crushed when a faithful friend lies to us, and divorce usually brings psychological trauma to both parties.

It's impossible to live where everyone gets exactly what he or she deserves. You live healthy all of your life, but one undetected cell contains cancer, and in your retirement years you have to go under the knife; and if that's not enough, you have to take radiation or chemotherapy. Where is the justice? Didn't you live healthy and do all the right things? Didn't you deprive yourself of fatty food and you never indulged in sweets or cigarettes or abusive alcohol? You've been the epitome of health, yet there's the fact of cancer. Why? There is no moral answer to the question of why. Cancer is the result of a wayward cell in your body, and it happens to many people, regardless of their righteousness or unrighteousness.

If every time we did good God rewarded us, wouldn't that make God like a dog trainer who gives a "goody" each time the dog performs what is required? It would be a fair world, but that's not the world that God has created. If we were always rewarded because we did right, we would become righteous for our own gain, and that would cause our selfish motives to contaminate the very act of goodness. We would love God because He is a gift-giver; we would not love Him for who He is and His love for us.

God wants us to love Him freely. Look at the angels: they worship God continually, crying, "Holy, Holy, Holy." They have to worship God. The angels do not have the free choice to reject God or disobey Him. They are frozen into righteousness. So they magnify God with their praise, but God knows it doesn't come from the free choice of their nature, for angels do not have free choice.

So God created creatures—Adam and Eve—and gave them free will to do what they wanted. Can you imagine the sovereign Creator of the universe making a man in His own image, and then allowing that man the free will to either love God or reject Him? If you can't imagine that picture, then you don't understand the nature of God.

Jesus said, "The Father seeks people to worship Him" (John 4:24, *ELT*). This means that God is seeking people to worship Him of their own free will.

The End of Job's Suffering

So look again at Job: wasn't Satan telling God that Job didn't have a free will to worship God? Job was just like a dog being trained; he served God for the "goodies." Isn't that what psychologists call conditioning? If you get an electric shock, you are negatively conditioned to jump or avoid pain. If you get a chocolate chip cookie, you are positively conditioned to smile, say thank you, or to please the giver so you can get another chocolate chip cookie.

Of course God sat in heaven listening to everything that Job and his critics said. And at the end of the book, God speaks: "My wrath is aroused against you and your two friends [Job's critics]." Why is God angry? "For you have not spoken of Me what is right, as My servant Job has" (Job 42:7).

God wanted worship from Job; therefore, He said to the three uncles, "Therefore take unto you now seven bullocks and seven rams, and go to my servant Job, and offer up for yourselves a burnt offering; and my servant Job shall pray for you: for him will I accept" (Job 42:8, *KJV*). Wow! Learn four lessons from the book of Job.

First, God wants worship for people, both the sinners (the unclean) and the ones only accused of sin (Job). God wasn't concerned with why Job suffered, but God honored his faithfulness in pain. God wanted worship from that man. After you suffer according to the will of God, God will want worship from you.

Second, the one suffering was called "my servant." Maybe—just maybe—your positive reaction to your suffering is the way God wants you to serve Him.

Third, the sufferer had to pray for his critics—the ones who were hypocritical. "My servant Job will pray for you . . . lest I deal with you after your folly." So when you're in the hospital bed, maybe you're supposed to pray for your healthy friends. Maybe we have it reversed when we think it's the duty of the healthy people to pray for the sick.

Fourth, notice the one in whom God delighted. It was not in the "visiting comforters." God said, "For him [Job] I accept."

God was much closer to the hurting Job than He was to the healthy "pastoral visitors."

This picture of Job changes everything. Job was the one spiritually whole—even though he hurt. Job was the mentor; his uncles were the learners. Job was the strong one; they were the weak.

So if you're on a bed of pain, maybe God wants you to encourage those who come to visit you—rather than the reverse.

So where does that bring us with our suffering and pain? When we lie suffering in the hospital bed, we have the free will to react any way we choose. Most people choose to complain, "Why me?" which means they question God's sovereignty. Or in their suffering they cry out, "Why this?" which is a question of God's plan for our life, because we think He has purposefully hurt us. And finally in our pain we cry, "Why now?" which is a question of God's timing.

All three questions center on God's integrity. Does God know what He's doing? Does God care what He's doing? Is God responsible for what He's doing—causing my pain?

Make a Hospital Room a Sanctuary

One day in the hospital bed, I hurt so badly that tears came to my eyes. Grabbing a tissue, I quickly wiped my eyes. I didn't want my wife to see me crying.

I hit the morphine button but I didn't realize that the nurse hadn't attached the button to the morphine bottle. I was not getting any pain relief. I kept wondering, *Why doesn't the morphine take away the pain?* I wondered if my pain was so unusually severe that morphine couldn't shut down the nerve endings.

In my deepest pain, I did something that completely took my mind off the pain and I stopped hurting. At other places in this book, I say that diversion takes our mind off the pain so that we don't hurt.

I chose to make my hospital room a sanctuary. I had prayed for God to help me through the pain, but my prayers bounced off the ceiling. That morning I had read the Scriptures, yet the words stuck to the pages. On other occasions the words of the

Scripture leaped off the pages into my heart and set my soul singing. But not that morning. In my pain the words of Scripture didn't move; they just lay there, denying me any comfort or help.

Then I remembered how to make any room a sanctuary. Remember, a sanctuary is where God dwells, and when we worship God, He comes to receive our worship. So I started worshiping God, knowing that "The Lord dwells in the center of the praises of His people" (Ps. 22:3, *ELT*).

The movie *Field of Dreams* made a statement that became a slogan for many Americans: "If you build it, they will come." In the movie, an Iowa farmer heard voices that told him that if he built a ball field, the ancient ball players would come to play on his field. Let's take that phrase and apply it to our relationship with God. *If you worship God, He will come to receive your praise.* Why? Because the Father seeks worship!

So in my hospital room of pain, I began worshiping God; and before I knew it, I was caught up in a love-relationship with God Himself.

I quit thinking about myself, and the diversion worked. I forgot about my pain and suffering. All I could think about was God Himself and how I needed to worship Him in so many different ways.

I have written three books on the names of God (*The Names of Jesus*[3], *My Father's Names*[4], and the Gold Medallion award-winning book *The Names of the Holy Spirit*[5]), so I began worshiping Jesus by as many names as I could remember. I worshiped the Father by as many different names, titles and metaphors as I could remember. So I worshiped Father, Son and Holy Spirit through their many different names, calling on them by their many different names and thanking them for what each name represented.

——————— WRAP-UP ———————

Next time you're in pain, try to make your hospital room a sanctuary. And even if you're not in the hospital, you can make any place a sanctuary by worshiping God. Because when you worship God, He will come to receive your worship, and that'll become your sanctuary. He comes so that He might receive the *worthship* that is due to Him.

Notes

1. Rick Warren, *The Purpose Driven Life*, "When God Seems Distant," chapter 14 (Grand Rapids, MI: Zondervan, 2002), pp. 107-113.

2. Aaron Burgess quotes Chuck Swindoll in *When Pain Is Prolonged* sermon. http:// sermoncentral.com/sermon.asp?SermonID=80723&ContributorID=6747 (accessed April 2006).

3. Elmer L. Towns, *The Names of Jesus* (Denver, CO: Accent Books, 1987). There are over 700 names, titles, metaphors, offices and figures of speech in the Bible that refer to Jesus. You could spend all day worshiping the Savior with His many names. This book is available free at www.elmertowns.com.

4. Elmer Towns, *My Father's Names* (Ventura, CA: Regal Books, 1991). There are over 100 various titles to the Father.

5. Elmer Towns, *Names of the Holy Spirit* (Ventura, CA: Regal Books, 1994). This was the first book ever written on the names of the Holy Spirit. When I began writing this book, I didn't know of a dozen names in Scripture for the Holy Spirit. I prayed and asked the Holy Spirit to help me find as many as possible. This book lists 126 different names for the Holy Spirit. This book won the Gold Medallion Book Award presented by ECPA (Evangelical Christian Publishers Association) and CBA (Christian Booksellers Association).

15

TRANSFORMATION

SUFFERING AS A CHANGE AGENT

Bodily pain affects man as a whole down to the deepest layers of his moral being. It forces him to face again the fundamental questions of his fate, of his attitude toward God and fellow man, of his individual and collective responsibility and of the sense of his pilgrimage on earth.

POPE PIUS XII[1]

God may use suffering, but God is not the original cause of suffering; He is too good to hurt His people. But through suffering His people can be transformed. And what is the transformation? Sometimes we suffer physically (major surgery), whereby we suffer before we get healthy. Sometimes inward suffering (mental suffering) makes us stronger on the inside.

Suffering is neither good nor bad, and the person who suffers is neither fortunate nor unfortunate. So what I'm saying is that suffering is morally neutral.

We must remember that sin is not a thing, even though some think a cigarette is sin, or a shot of whiskey is evil. No! Evil never resides in things; evil is a choice.

When Adam and Eve chose to eat the fruit of the garden—the fruit was not sin—their sin was disobedience to God. And their disobedience had disastrous results. They had been made in the image of God, which involved their intellect, emotion, will, plus their self-perception and self-direction. It was not sin when Adam emotionally craved the fruit of the tree of the center of the garden. It became sin when our parents chose to listen to Satan and carry out their ill-conceived plan.

Let's bring this discussion down to our pain and suffering. The bottom line is that we are responsible for our actions and reactions. Our suffering is never beneficial in itself; how we react to our suffering is the key to whether we benefit or not.

When you are knocked to the ground, how will you react to the blow that brought you to your knees? In a moment you hold your head and ask, "Why me? Why this? Why now?" It is then that you have the choice of learning something from the "punch" that landed you on the ground. The right decision when you are hurting and lying on the ground may determine the way you live the rest of your life. Lots of people are knocked down and bounce back up simply because they want to get up.

The winners of this life are knocked down like the losers, but winners learn something from the blow and determine to be a better person. Sometimes they make better choices so they won't be knocked down again. When that happens, the blow becomes a transforming action.

We suffer when we break something. It hurts to break an arm, a finger, or a leg. Obviously, the act of breaking has its pain, and the pain tells us to stop doing what we are doing so we won't cause more harm to our body. Pain motivates us to seek help. Pain keeps us inactive during the healing process so that we won't further injure ourselves. So pain helps us physically.

What about psychological pain or mental pain? Perhaps you have a "wrong" way of doing things, and you need to break that habit. Perhaps you have an old destructive routine that is a comfortable routine, but you have no power to stop that routine. So God breaks your spirit, like breaking a bone. There's pain in your heart and soul. Now the question is this: Will you make a decision to learn from that pain that comes from brokenness or will you go back to the old way of doing things? When things break in your life, maybe God is trying to teach you a new routine.

Remember, there's a cross and crown in the Christian life. Jesus commands us, "If anyone desires to come after Me, let him deny himself, and take up his cross daily, and follow Me" (Luke 9:23). We become His disciples by obedient following, a daily following, a transformed following. Are you following Jesus? If not, watch out! A cross may be in your future.

When you think of a cross, think of the agonizing death that Jesus suffered. This involves thirst, tearing of the flesh, being pierced by a spear, humiliation, and the realization that your friends have abandoned you. Is that the pain that is in the future for you?

Most Christians want to wear the crown because they've been promised the crown of life. Do you remember the words of Paul: "Finally, there is laid up for me the crown of righteousness, which the Lord, the righteous Judge, will give to me on that Day, and not to me only but also to all who have loved His appearing" (2 Tim. 4:8)?

To get the crown, you must first bear the cross!

The cross is heavy and carrying it saps our energy. A cross is humiliating in that it crushes our self-importance. The cross is rejection, so maybe we will lose some friends. A cross is agonizingly heavy so that every muscle in your body aches and you feel that every bone in your body is going to be broken. Nevertheless, you must take up your cross with all its difficulties if you're going to get a crown.

Let's look at the decision we make when we suffer. The very first thing we must do is yield ourselves into the hands of God. Isn't yielding a choice? The next time you suffer pain, yield to the purpose and plan of God. Now remember, there is nothing good in pain itself; but if through pain we learn to walk more carefully, then pain is good.

Yieldedness is an unusual thing. Very seldom do we give up our rights! Yieldedness produces the doctrine of opposite results. And what do I mean by that? Didn't Jesus say, "But many who are first will be last, and the last first" (Matt. 19:30; Mark 10:31)? Didn't Jesus say that we would be exalted if we humble ourselves (see Luke 14:11; 18:14)? Didn't Jesus set a small child in front of us and tell us to become childlike if we wanted to enter His kingdom (see Matt. 19:14; Mark 10:14; Luke 18:16)? Didn't Jesus say that those who rule must first serve (see Luke 22:26)?

So what does the principle of opposite results teach? It teaches that we must go down if we want to rise. It teaches that we must become nothing if we want to gain something. It teaches that we must be weak in order to be strong. It teaches that we must give up our rights to gain our privileges in heaven. And where is pain in the doctrine of opposite results? We must embrace our pain if we are to get strong. Pain forces us to choose to be transformed by our suffering, rather than choosing to be destroyed by it.

So next time you have a great reversal, and your dreams are crushed beyond repair, look around for the opportunity or a decision that could transform your life. Look at your pain though the eyes of God to see what He is doing in your life.

What Does God See?

1. God knows that our suffering will make us more dependent upon Him.
2. God knows that our suffering will cut us off from things and stuff, to make us cry out for Him.
3. God knows that suffering will whittle away at our sense of self-importance.
4. God knows that our suffering will teach us patience, and patience will teach us faith, and faith will produce character.
5. God knows that suffering brings us to the point where we are willing to listen to the gospel or to His plan for our life.
6. Finally, God knows that when we suffer, we will be willing to answer His call and do His will.

And after we suffer, we can then be blessed of God. Isn't that the opposite of what we expect? We think the blessing of God is feeling good, getting ahead, prospering, and having a happy life. Notice what Jesus said about blessedness in the Beatitudes: "Blessed are the poor in spirit" (Matt. 5:3). And who are the poor? Those who have had all their earthly goods snatched from them so that they suffer the pain of poverty. "Blessed are they that mourn" (Matt. 5:4). And who are those that mourn? Those who are hurt and afflicted. "Blessed are those who are persecuted for righteousness' sake . . . and blessed are you when they [men] revile and persecute you, and say all kinds of evil against you falsely for My sake" (Matt. 5:10-11). Think of all the pain that goes with persecution. There is the emotional pain of embarrassment, then there's the psychological pain of loss, and finally, the physical pain of beating, depravity or torture of the body.

Jesus didn't give the normal hospital platitude, which is, "You'll feel better tomorrow." To be blessed was not to feel better. No, through all the pain that the people were suffering, He was teaching them the principle of opposite results, which means, "His strength is made perfect in weakness" (2 Cor. 12:9). And what does this mean? This means that there is a lesson in pain for us to learn something from opposite results.

——————— WRAP-UP ———————

Notice how the principle of opposite results applied in Jesus' life: "For though He was crucified in weakness, yet He lives by the power of God" (2 Cor. 13:4). Jesus went through the embarrassment of a trial followed by the pain of the cross, but today He enjoys the blessedness of sitting at the right hand of the heavenly Father.

Now apply the lesson of opposite results to your life. "We also are weak in Him, but we shall live with Him by the power of God" (2 Cor. 13:4). This means that our life is "sown in weakness, and . . . raised in power" (1 Cor. 15:43). Our example is Jesus, who got resurrection strength from the pain of suffering. So our strength is made perfect in weakness. We learn from pain that weakness leads to victory so that our sufferings become "chariot wheels" to ride over the enemy that oppresses us.

Note

1. Pope Pius XII to a group of international heart specialists, news summaries September 1, 1956. http://www.bartleby.com/63/47/4247.html (accessed March 2006).

Section Four

TECHNICAL VIEWS OF PAIN

Pain is hunger; it's that gnawing emptiness that demands, "Feed me." Nothing takes hunger away except food; and nothing takes pain away but a return to health. You can mask your hunger pangs only for a time, but like pain that's covered with morphine or aspirin, it'll come back. If hunger gets too intense, you'll die—the same with pain.

Hunger saps your strength and takes away your initiative. Not only will you lose interest in doing the fun things of life, but also you'll lose your desire to do the necessary things of life like employment, cleaning the house and bathing. Then when you're desperately weak, you'll lose your ability to do these things.

Chapter 16 deals with the technical descriptions of pain and some things you can do to alleviate or block pain. Chapter 17 describes health—the goal you think is elusive when you're suffering. Thank God if you have the good health described here in this chapter.

16

PATHOLOGY

THERE ARE ALL KINDS OF PAIN

In pain you can be more meditative than in pleasure. Pleasure is more distracting. . . . Pleasure tends to make you unconscious; pleasure is a sort of oblivion, a forgetfulness. Pain is remembrance: you cannot forget pain. If there is pain, use it as an awareness, as meditation, as a sharpening of the soul.

BHAGWAN SHREE RAJNEESH
(Indian Spiritual leader, 1931–1990)[1]

What's the most obvious thing about a person in pain? Pain hurts! What's the most obvious reaction to pain? We hate it—if we're normal.

There is no way around it. When you hurt, you hurt. You don't want consolation, or devotional thoughts, or Bible reading; you might not even want someone to visit you. What you want is to stop hurting.

Now the things mentioned above can help. When we read the Bible, we learn God's plan for our life and that gives us hope to live beyond our pain. When we pray, it also gives us hope that God will heal us quicker than usual, or heal us altogether. Sometimes devotional thoughts from a visiting pastor will divert our thinking about pain and that helps.

Look how *Webster* defines pain: "localized physical suffering associated with body disorder, or disease or injury." Therefore, pain is suffering. *Webster* gives a second definition that describes how pain affects us: "a basic bodily sensation, induced by noxious stimulus, received by naked nerve endings, characterized by physical discomfort and typically leading to evasive actions."[2] That definition basically says, "Pain hurts and we ought to do something about it."

There are two kinds of pain. The first is physical pain. The Bible describes the suffering that came upon Phinehas's wife when she was about to give birth to a son: "her pains came upon her" (1 Sam. 4:19). Obviously, this is reference to labor pains.

The second is mental pain, which gives us discomfort or suffering when we think about what happened, or is about to happen. The Bible speaks of mental agony when it says, "To know this, it was too painful for me" (Ps. 73:16, *KJV*).

Notice the interrelationship between the two: your physical pain can sometimes cause mental anguish. For instance, you hear a baby cry and worry what is going to happen to the child, or the doctor sees a spot on your lungs in the X-ray and you are fearful that you might have cancer. People who are prone to fear end up neurotic. So that means their physical symptoms probably lead to mental pain.

But there's an opposite to that. Sometimes mental pain produces physical actions that hurt. Perhaps you worry about a job interview, or the boss has called you in and you fear you might be fired. Your mental suffering could lead to a physical headache, or even stomach nausea so that you might throw up. In this case, mental pain has led to physical pain.

This is described by two books that C. S. Lewis wrote. In the first, *The Problem of Pain* (1940), Lewis describes the problem of physical pain. This is a philosophical treatment whereby Lewis explains the nature of pain, and why God allows it in our life.[3] Twenty-one years later, after his wife died, C. S. Lewis wrote *A Grief Observed*, which examines the mental pain he felt when his wife died.[4]

Kinds of Physical Pain

1. *Acute pain* is something that strikes immediately, such as when we touch a hot surface or the skin is puncture by a needle or knife. Acute pain is intense, demanding, and has a sharp sensation.

When my granddaughter heard me dictating this part of the book, she thought I said "a cute pain." There is nothing about an acute pain that is cute. Acute pain is ugly, nauseating, demanding and instantaneously harmful.

People with acute pain don't need a counselor; they need aspirin, or a prescription for non-steroidal anti-inflammatory drugs (NSAIDs) from a doctor to stop the pain. Sure you need prayer, and prayer may stop the pain, but suppose it doesn't? Then you ought to pray that the doctor makes the right diagnosis and that you get the right medicine, and that God gives you grace to suffer through this acute pain.

2. *Chronic pain* also is called *dull pain* and is usually associated with disease in the body such as arthritis, problems in the organs, or even cancer itself. This pain is difficult to analyze and even more difficult to locate and treat.

Usually chronic pain lasts longer than acute pain. Whereas acute pain calls instant attention to a problem so that you get medical treatment immediately, chronic pain outlives that immediate warning. Chronic pain no longer helps the body to prevent injury; all that chronic pain does is hurt. That's because chronic pain lasts beyond the cause of the pain.

3. *Cutaneous pain*. This is usually pain associated with an injury to the skin—a very localized kind of pain. So when you cut yourself, or slam your finger in a car door, or get hit sharply some place on your skin, you have cutaneous pain. You know where you hurt, and immediately you begin to rub it, because rubbing does divert pain from its intensity—rubbing intercepts raw nerve impulses from being transferred to the brain. Also, when you put pressure on a wound, or apply ice or heat, these are diversionary techniques that keep nerve endings from sending messages to the brain.

Pain is usually associated with any type of skin damage in the body. However, you don't have pain receptors in every part of your body, so you won't have pain in every part of your body. As an illustration, visceral organs—internal within the body cavity—can be cut by a doctor without generating pain. However, when the doctor cuts the skins of the body cavity with a scalpel, it creates intense pain.

There are several organs in the body that are not stimulated by pain, e.g., the liver, the lungs and the alveoli.

4. *Somatic pain.* This is a dull, poorly localized pain we have somewhere in our body or deep in our muscles of the arms or legs. This could be a pain in the ligaments, bones, blood vessels, or internal organs. This pain is hard to diagnose and even more difficult to treat.

5. *Visceral pain.* The viscera are internal organs in the body cavity, so this is pain that comes from the organs of the body inside the body cavity. The cause is usually extremely hard to diagnose and the doctor has to use a variety of investigative treatments to examine inside the body, whether he uses an investigative laparoscope, diagnostic abdominal navel probe, or heart catheterization tool.

6. *Neuropathy pain.* This occurs when we receive an injury to our nervous system—perhaps on the spinal column, neck or brain; or there's been physical damage to muscles, blood vessels, or even the bone cavity itself. As a result, damage is done to the nerves and these nerve endings send pain impulses to the brain.

7. *Phantom pain* is usually associated with amputees. As an illustration, when a limb has been lost, people still feel pain in a lost finger or pain in a part of the body that is no longer there. The limb has been amputated but the pain response is still signaled to the brain as if it is being damaged or hurt.

8. *Pain receptors* are located in the skin, and for the most part, they initiate the pain that's transmitted to the brain. The nerve fibers have nerve endings that can be excited by three types of stimuli: chemical, physical or mechanical. These nerve fibers transmit an electrical impulse from the tissues to the spinal cord via nerve tracks.

There are three types of nerve tracks: A delta fibres are larger and they conduct pain more quickly because they identify well-localized pain and communicate it rapidly; the second smaller C fibres usually respond to chemical or mechanical stimulation; and the third is a quick sensation of pain that first hits the skin followed by a dull or throbbing sensation.

Behavioral Reaction to Suffering

* Refusal to take pain medication
* Refusal of assistance from care givers
* Power struggles with family
* Puts self in unsafe position
* Frantically seeks advice from everyone
* Active forms of self-harm
* Lack of engagement with activities that bring relief or comfort
* Withdrawal/isolation
* Statements about "not wanting to be a burden"
* Refuses spiritual leader or gives up faith

When pain enters the spinal cord, it is communicated to the brain by two different pathways. The first influences your conscious sensation of pain; you know it hurts because the impulse hits the brain stem and your thalamus to create an immediate sensation of "hurt."

Doctors have found that the pain threshold—reception of pain—is relatively similar in all people; however, you can educate your pain threshold so that eventually you won't react to pain as severely as previously. As an illustration, children react more violently to pain than do adults, which is another way of saying that children hurt more when a dentist drills in their teeth than an adult. I've read this in a book, but the dental procedure still hurts when the dentist drills on my teeth, even though I'm an adult.

There are some other things that affect your pain threshold, such as depression and anxiety. Depression lowers your severity of pain, while anxiety heightens the intensity of pain. Anger or excitement can also temporarily lessen the intensity of pain.

Also, people who understand pain can educate themselves to raise their pain tolerance threshold because they know how pain is perceived, and they don't react violently to it, as they did when they are startled, or they see themselves hurt, pierced or cut.

Kinds of Mental Pain

There are many different elements of mental pain and this list is not even exhaustive. Probably you can think of some things that I have left out:

1. *Physical death.*
The worst impact that death has on surviving family members is that they have lost a loved one and they are left with an emptiness or "hole in the heart." The dead person no longer can fill in the empty spaces of life that they once did, so we mourn or grieve when there is death. Mourning is an internal suffering, grieving is outward crying and weeping. Notice Abraham displayed both these pain emotions, "Abraham came to mourn for Sarah and to weep for her" (Gen. 23:2).

2. *Loss of dreams or plans.*
You may have a dream of building a home or starting a business or any other dream that makes life meaningful. When that dream

is crushed, it brings pain; and the greater the dream grips you, the greater will be your pain when your dream is crushed.

Israel had left slavery in Egypt and they were looking forward to entering the Promised Land, a land "flowing with milk and honey" (Exod. 3:8). Each family would live in a home, plant a garden, and it would be theirs. But Israel constantly rebelled against God, and finally at Kadesh-Barnea they refused to go into the Promised Land. What happened when they got the news of God's judgment? "When the people heard [they couldn't go into Cana] . . . they mourned" (Exod. 33:4). They had chosen their destiny by rejecting God's will, and now they were mourning because they had to suffer the consequences.

3. *Memory.*

Painful memory brings pain. When we remember our love for a departed loved one, we mourn. When we remember the stupid things we have done, our embarrassment brings about pain. We remember the good things we had in life, but when they are gone, we weep and yearn for the past. What was Nehemiah's pain when he remembered the past life in Jerusalem? "I sat down and wept, and mourned [for many] days" (Neh. 1:4). Nehemiah wept because Solomon's temple was destroyed; God's people couldn't return there for the sacrifice of sins, nor could they enter God's presence to worship Him.

4. *The conviction of sin.*

The Holy Spirit convicts the world of sin (see John 16:8). The word "convicts" comes from the Latin root "to cause to see." The Holy Spirit causes us to see the stupidity of our sin and we feel bad. We remember that we offended God or we've hurt other people, and we've gone against our conscience. What should we do when we are convicted of our sin? The Bible tells us, "Lament, and mourn, and weep" (Jas. 4:9). This anguish is good, because weeping over the pain of sin motivates us to seek God's peace.

5. *Repentance of sin.*

People usually repent because they hurt—internally—and they don't want to continue hurting themselves. Zechariah reminds Israel of their repentance: "When you fasted and mourned . . . even those seventy years" (Zech. 7:5). He was reminding the people that for 70 years in Babylon, they couldn't go home to the Promised Land, they couldn't worship in the Temple, and they weren't free; they were slaves. So for 70 years they hurt spiritually and probably every year of those 70 years they told God how sorry they were for their sins. Yet, God didn't immediately take away their pain, nor did He reward their repentance with relief; Israel had to suffer the entire 70 years before they could return to the Promised Land.

6. *Anticipated death.*

Sometimes we mourn when we know a loved one is dying or when we realize that we will die. The doctors may tell you that you have cancer, and at best six months to live. What happens in the next six months? Some people go out on a high note, and do everything they can to fulfill their dreams. Others go out on a low note, mourning over what they think is premature death. The Bible describes this: "And you mourn at last, when your flesh and your body are consumed" (Prov. 5:11). "At last" means when we take our last breath and the last of life is lived.

7. *Deprivation.*

Sometimes we mourn because we can't have what we want: we want a certain job at work and don't get it; we want to marry a certain mate, but we are turned down. We want to get out of jail, or to buy a better house, or provide more food for the family, or anything that we can't physically have. The Bible calls this "The sufferings of this present time are not worthy [to be compared] with the glory which shall be" (Rom. 8:18).

8. *Identificational pain.*

Sometimes it is not we who have pain, but we hurt because someone we love is suffering. When we identify with them and pray for them, we feel their pain. These words are easy to say, but not always appreciated: "I know how you feel!" Usually when someone says that to me I think, "No, you don't know how I feel." So I rebel at what I call intrusive compassion.

But there are those real times when I know someone is hurting and I hurt with them. Maybe I don't know all they are going through, but I still hurt.

Suppose you are with a person in an automobile accident, and while you are not injured, your friend is seriously injured. You feel their pain, you weep, and you panic. You go through emotional agony because your friend is injured.

Technically, every Christian should feel pain when he hears of another Christian's suffering. Paul uses the analogy of the body and says, "And if one member suffers, all the members suffer with [it]" (1 Cor. 12:26). Anybody who has been in the hospital knows that one incision on any part of your body, whether toe, stomach or eye, hurts the entire body. When my friends suffer, I suffer with them.

Alleviation of Pain

There is more than one way to alleviate pain. Pain can be lessened psychologically and physiologically. As an illustration, the reduction of anxiety—psychologically—may lessen the amount of pain you feel. This means that you may take a lesser amount of pain medication to alleviate pain when you feel good about a situation.

Sometimes when we are hit on the arm or leg, we immediately rub the spot to relieve the pain. The rubbing disconnects the pain fibres from the synapse. The pain sensation is not completely communicated to your brain, so you don't feel it as badly. The same thing can be done by applying heat, which takes away the pain when you smash your finger with a hammer. Heat disconnects the fibres from the synapse; the same thing occurs with cold-water application. When you smash your finger, you sometimes put ice on it to alleviate the pain.

Sometimes rest alleviates the pain so that when the mind is at ease, you stop thinking about the pain and it does not hurt as much. You get the same alleviation when you go to sleep.

There are opiates that are pain-relieving medications. Some doctors use opium—the dried juice of an opium poppy. This is one of the oldest analgesics to deal with pain. Morphine is another pain reliever to block excessive pain. This narcotic alkaloid mimics the endorphins by attaching themselves to the receptors and blocking, or reducing, the activation of pain neurons.

Be careful about these opiates; these contain addictive substances. In the process of healing or alleviating pain, the patient develops tolerance to the opiate; therefore the patient requires progressively greater doses to reduce the level of pain. What's happening? They are building up an addiction to that opiate. As a result, doctors seldom prescribe these narcotics for long-term therapy. They are usually prescribed to lessen pain immediately after surgery or to treat patients who have terminal cancer when addiction is not an issue, because death may be imminent.

The bark of willow trees contains the active ingredient salicin, which has been used by doctors throughout history to relieve pain. The modern non-narcotic analgesic salicylates are basically what we call aspirin. They are less potent than opiates, and they're non-addictive. Aspirin blocks the conversion of arachidic acid (a fatty acid) that enhances sensitivity of pain.

There are certain psychiatric medications that could be used to treat pain. These are antidepressants and tranquilizers. Usually, these are prescribed to those whose pain is thought to be primarily psychological. These medicines alter the perception of pain and help to reduce anxiety. There are other ways to deal with psychological pain—hypnosis and psychotherapy, which gives psychological expectation of relief as a potential pain reliever.

Emotional Reaction

- Anger
- Loss of hope and meaning

- Restlessness/agitation/anxiety
- Denial of illness or of reality of prognosis
- Shame or guilt
- Grief
- Fear
- Powerlessness and loss of control
- Depression/discouragement
- Nightmares or dread

Some pain is treated by electrical stimulation through electrodes placed under the skin. As a result the peripheral nerve endings are not able to affect the nerve fibres that generate the pain. This is similar to the same process described earlier where you relieve pain by rubbing the painful area, applying heat, or compressing it. When you hit your finger with a hammer, you grab the finger and hold it as tightly as possible, compressing, to inhibit the pain.

People born with insensitivity to pain usually don't live long and usually suffer numerous ailments. Why? Their brain does not have any nociceptive tissues; hence they cannot experience pain. Because pain does not alert them to a problem they may have in their body, they may continue their action with a broken bone, causing more damage or producing dangerous levels of inflammation. They may have a disease but they don't know it. So they don't treat it, thus causing more damage or they die prematurely.

WRAP-UP

You can analyze your suffering but that doesn't make the pain go away. You can explain to the patient why he/she is hurting but that doesn't usually help. What they want is relief! So this chapter may not help anyone in pain, but maybe we can do something about it if we at least know enough about our pain that we know what will relieve it.

Notes

1. Bhagwan Shree Rajneesh. http://members.surfeu.fi/wpk/links/other/qts.htm, (accessed April 2006).

2. *Merriam-Webster Online Dictionary,* s.v. "pain." http://www.m-w.com/dictionary/pain, (accessed March 2006).

3. C. S. Lewis, *The Problem of Pain* (San Francisco, CA: HarperSanFrancisco, 2001).

4. C. S. Lewis, *A Grief Observed,* reprint edition (San Francisco, CA: HarperSanFrancisco, 1989).

17

HEALTH

HEALTH IS THE ABSENCE OF
DISEASE OR PAIN

*Never continue in a job you don't enjoy. If you're happy in what
you're doing, you'll like yourself, you'll have inner peace.
And if you have that, along with physical health, you will have
had more success than you could possibly have imagined.*

JOHNNY CARSON,
U.S. COMEDIAN AND TELEVISION HOST
(1925–2005)[1]

While this book is concerned about pain and its effect on your
life, let's look carefully at the opposite of pain—good health.
And what is good health? First, the obvious and insufficient
answer is, "Health is the absence of disease." Beyond that, some
have defined health as physical, mental, emotional, economic
and spiritual well-being. But there are other aspects that this
definition leaves out. When you are healthy, you fulfill social
roles, such as being a good parent, performing tasks satisfac-
torily, being gainfully employed, and fostering good marriage
relationships. There are other aspects to health, such as enjoying
supportive social networks with both friends and strangers, as
well as feeling the value of love and worth from other people.

However, for this chapter, health is defined as "a dynamic
state of wellbeing characterized by a physical, mental and social

potential, which satisfies the demands of a life commensurate with age, culture, and personal responsibilities."[2]

On the other side, pain is a physical, emotional and psychological phenomenon that alerts the person to danger in his environment or to the body and produces negative attitudes and adjustments to life. In other words, *pain hurts.*

Everybody wants to function in a healthy way, but many times forces attack the body and cause it to malfunction. When this happens, pain sets in to alert the body that something is wrong.

Everyone received the embryonic pattern for their body at the moment of conception, and that highly complex mechanism is an amazing machine that makes a person self-productive, self-corrective and self-supportive. So when does the body have good health? When it is able to function the way God designed it. So you should be just as concerned about your physical health as your spiritual health.

However, no one is physically perfect, just as no one is spiritually able to live without sin (see 1 John 1:8-10). Everyone has some defects in their body; a few people have defects that are life threatening, others may be debilitating, and still others may be just irritating or slightly limiting.

No matter what defect you have, most people learn to live with their defects or limitations. As an example, notice how some blind people learn to live with this handicap. Some have compensated in other areas and have made outstanding contributions to life, such as Fanny Crosby who wrote many hymns and is considered one of the most prolific hymn writers of all time, writing over 8,000 hymns and living to the age of 95. She considered blindness her friend: "It seemed intended by the blessed providence of God that I should be blind all my life, and I thank him for the dispensation. If perfect earthly sight were offered me tomorrow I would not accept it. I might not have sung hymns to the praise of God if I had been distracted by the beautiful and interesting things about me."[3]

Eat Your Way to Good Health

Diet makes a realistic contribution to a healthy body. The body should not only work well and work in harmony with all its parts, but also it needs proper nutrition and energy to continue operating effectively. God has put two things in the body to help us maintain good health. First is the sense of taste so that we eat that which is enjoyable and good for us. Second, God builds within the human "distastes" that keep us from eating that which is not healthy or may even be harmful to the body. But in general, most people seem to know what foods their bodies need to function properly in a healthy way.

But there are some foods that may taste good but are unhealthy for the body. These include foods that are salty, fatty or sugary, and other products that may be addictive, such as alcohol or cigarettes. The use of these may lead to pain, discomfort, limited physical ability and decreased dexterity and flexibility—perhaps even to premature death.

Exercise Your Way to Good Health

Good health is also defined by exercise. The human body was created to be physically active, not passive. The human heart must pump fast once in a while to keep its muscle tone as well as unclog arteries throughout the venous system. Our lungs need exercise so that their entire capacity is healthy and usable. If you had a racecar, you wouldn't drive it to work each day; it's designed for high-speed racetracks. Without driving it at a higher speed, you would eventually destroy its engine productivity. The same with a dump truck. You don't put it on a racetrack and try to drive it 150 miles per hour in a 500-mile race. Again, you would destroy its engine's usability and longevity.

What does all this mean? Exercise is important to maintain physical health.

Protect Your Health

Your body is constantly under attack and God has built defenses within the physical body to protect itself against these attacks. As an illustration: If you ingest germs, poison (non-deadly) or viruses, they are screened out by the liver, kidneys and spleen. So don't be horrified when a baby picks up a germ-filled cookie out of a litter box; God has built in a filtering process that's tied to the health of the baby.

The body is also attacked by germs, bacteria, viruses and molds. These enemies not only bring sickness and pain, but also they make their home in the body to destroy our cells and many times release poison that negatively affects the body.

It is said that cleanliness is next to godliness, but it can also be said that cleanliness is next to health. By keeping the body clean—washing hands after using the bathroom—you protect yourself against disease. At the same time, the body is constantly working to create internal defenses against specific bacteria and viruses. Many professionals say that being too clean can be unhealthy because you may not develop accurate defenses needed to maintain health.

Injury is another area that causes pain. If you're hit by an object that breaks a bone, or the outer skin is penetrated, or you're attacked by an animal, any one of these can cause pain and danger to the body's health. Injury comes from an accident over which we have no control. At other times it is our carelessness or ignorance that results in injury and pain.

As suggested earlier, ingesting poison can bring sickness, pain and physical deterioration. And all poison does not come into our system through what we eat. Sometimes poison gets to us through the subtle influence of the environment by smog and other poisons traveling through the atmosphere. Environmental poisoning is usually unavoidable; however, cigarette smoke, alcohol, and illegal drugs are potential poisons we ingest into our systems, and they shorten life, detract from our physical strength, beauty and/or agility—producing an unhealthy body.

The Body Heals Itself

After you become sick, the body heals itself by fighting any disease or injury it has suffered. The healthier the body, the easier and quicker it heals itself. Most think drugs prescribed by the doctor make us well. But that's not true. Prescription drugs fight infection and doctors cut away disease in surgery. The most natural part of health is natural healing when the body heals itself. And what is the goal of healing? It's to get the body functioning as it's designed to function. Therefore, give as much attention to good health, exercise, nutrition and sleep as you give to pain remedies and pain control (reduction).

More and more researchers are discovering that spirituality leads to a healthy life. They find that faith provides people with a sense of purpose so that when they face tough situations—including pain—their spiritual convictions help them fight anxiety, helplessness and depression. Spiritual convictions give meaning to life and order their physical and mental responses to pain and suffering. Spiritual convictions give people a sense of control over their destiny.[4]

And how does spirituality affect health? "Accumulating research suggests that the positive emotions (happiness, contentment, joy, etc.) are associated with a functioning healthy immune system."[5] One study found that depressed women who were suffering from breast cancer had fewer immune system cells and weaker overall immune functioning when compared to non-depressed women with breast cancer.[6]

Why is that? Your immune system is designed to seek out and kill cancer cells; so if you have fewer immune system cells, you are much more likely to encourage cancer or allow it to grow dangerously.

So don't think the minister visiting in the hospital is just spiritual handholding, or when friends drop by to cheer up a sick person that they are just exercising the power of positive thinking. Spiritual therapy is not window dressing. It's intimately tied to the efficiency of our immune system.

But spirituality is broader than just therapy to the sick person. You are generally physically healthy when your mind is spiritually healthy. The opposite is also true: When your mental or spiritual health declines, it eventually wears down the physical body. That has a reciprocal effect because when your health declines, you feel mentally down, thus creating a downward spiral toward suffering, physical limitations, and premature death.

The American Academy of Family Physicians says that two-thirds of office visits to family physicians are due to stress-related symptoms.[7]

As a matter of fact, the more a person does in life—multiple roles—tends to be a predictor of good health. Lois M. Verbrugge writes in *The Journal of Health and Social Behavior*, "Research has shown that employment and marriage are related to good physical health."[8] Her research shows that "married people have better health than any non-married group, and divorced or separated people had the poorest health."[9]

In summary, "Employment, marriage, and parenthood were linked with good health."[10]

———————— WRAP-UP ————————

Every suffering person wants pain relief; they want to be healthy again. But health is something most people don't think much about until they've lost it.

When you say health is the absence of disease and pain, that's only a negative definition. Health is good and positive—health is tying together our mental, emotional and social well-being to our physical well-being so that we can do all that we want to do.

Therefore, a healthy spiritual walk with God will contribute to our physical health. And when pain comes, it will help relieve some pain, and what suffering we can't eliminate, we can better deal with it.

Notice how Paul tied the will of God to our bodies. It all begins when you do a spiritual thing—you yield your body to God: "I plead with you to give your bodies to God . . . let God transform you into a new person by changing the way you think. Then you will know what God wants you to do, and you will know how good and pleasing and perfect his will really is" (Rom. 12:1-2, *NLT*).

Notes

1. Johnny Carson. http://www.quotationspage.com/quote/2965.html. (accessed May 2006).

2. J. Bircher, "Towards a Dynamic Definition of Health and Disease," *NCBI PubMed*. http://www.ncbi.nlm.nih.gov/entrez/query.fcgi?cmd=Retrieve&db=pubmed&dopt=Abstract&list_uids=16283496&itool=iconabstr&query_hl=1&itool=-pubmed_docsum (accessed May 2006).

3. *Frances Jane van Alystyne (Fanny Crosby), 1820-1915*, Hymn Writer. http://www.eaec.org/faithhallfame/fanny_crosby.htm (accessed May 2006).

4. *KidsHealth for Parents*, "How Can Spirituality Affect Your Family's Health?" http://www.kidshealth.org/parent/positive/family/spirituality.html (accessed May 2006).

5. *MentalHelp.net*, "Emotional Resilience, Physical Health Benefits." http://mentalhelp.net/poc/center_index.php?id=298 (accessed May 2006).

6. Ibid.

7. *APA Help Center*, "Mind/Body Health: Did You Know?" http://www.apahelpcenter.org/articles/article.php?id=103 (accessed May 2006).

8. Lois M. Verbrugge, "Multiple Roles and Physical Health of Women and Men," http://www.jstor.org/view/00221465/di976079/97p0325b/0 (accessed May 2006).

9. Ibid.

10. Ibid.

Afterthought

WHERE DO YOU GO FROM HERE?

Pain is a tool. Just as a craftsman has different chisels, saws and hammers for different jobs, so too the body uses different kinds of pain to accomplish different results in your body and mind. The best craftsman knows the minute differences between chisels and how to use each of them in his craft. So too your doctor knows the difference between various pains and what each of them means. So listen to your pains and listen to your doctor.

A craftsman gets in trouble when he tries to use a power hammer to do the job of a tack hammer. When he should be doing precise work in close quarters, the power hammer may split the wood and scar the surface. So learn the difference between your various pains.

God never sends pain, for a loving God cannot intentionally hurt anyone. But a loving doctor will make a painful incision on a chest cavity to save the life of a patient, just as a loving God will use pain to bring a person closer to Himself.

As I mentioned at the beginning of this book, death is not a subject that we think about much. At least not until we begin to suffer pain. And the more agonizing the pain, the more our real death pushes its way into our thinking.

Birth begins in pain and, just as assuredly, death ends in pain. But a painful death is not the climax to the story; there's more to follow. Because we have been saved by faith, we enter an eternity with God where there are no tears, no death and no pain.

So many people think that the Christian faith is a nice answer to death; we simply tell people we will go to be with Jesus. But it's more than that: the Bible says we overcome through death. Paul says, "Death is swallowed up in victory. O Death, where [is] your sting? O Hades, where [is] your victory?" (1 Cor. 15:54-55).

Pain and the purpose of God are a divine enigma. We don't always know what God is doing in our life, but He works all things together for His plans. All we can say is, "Oh, how great are God's riches and wisdom and knowledge! How impossible it is for us to understand his decisions and his ways! For who can know the Lord's thoughts? Who knows enough to give him advice? And who has given him so much that he needs to pay it back? For everything comes from him and exists by his power and is intended for his glory. All glory to him forever! Amen" (Rom. 11:33-36, *NLT*).